BLOCKCHAIN T?

REVOLUTION IN BUSINESS

EXPLAINED

DISCLAIMER

TABLE OF CONTENTS

7

THE HISTORY OF BLOCKCHAIN AND CRYPTOCURRENCY

Before we get started, I just wanted to talk about how excited I am about the potential future of blockchain technology; not just in business, but in every aspect of our daily lives. For the last decade, we have seen technology progress at breakneck speed. The advent of the internet, smartphone technology, video streaming, social media and online businesses have changed the face of the planet. However, there have been some downsides. Online privacy has taken a backseat for the average consumer, in the search of more business. Google and Facebook have decided that the pursuit of more clicks and revenue supersede our personal privacy.

Enter blockchain. Blockchain has the potential to give us more privacy through innovative encryption of our online activities. This could give businesses the info they need while protecting our privacy.

It also has the potential to revolutionize the way that transactions are made; eliminating the need for the middleman to check the authenticity of these transactions.

Now let's get started!

The Original Problem with Digital Transactions

Most Digital Purchases are Bank Transfers

Believe it or not, most digital transactions still occur like a normal bank transfer would nearly three decades ago. The only real difference is that it goes to a middleman before it is approved. You start a transaction since you want to pay for some item, the amount or, rather, the number associated with the amount is then sent to an auction clearing House. This clearing House talks with the associated bank you're giving the amount of money to and ensures there is an account to transfer to. That same clearing house also asks if the bank you're transferring from has an account with the number of the amount associated with it. Once it confirms both sides exist and you have money, it then commits the transaction.

As computers have gotten faster, these transactions have gotten faster as a result and so it's barely noticeable to the average consumer. However, essentially, you are doing a wire transfer every time you use a card, every time you use PayPal, and every time you use something like Google Pay.

Bank Transfers Are Tracked with Physical Items

The way that banks are able to do this is because they have an exchange rate. That is, they have a rate of which items can be exchanged in their program otherwise known as Fiat money. It is not the same exchange rate that is referred to when talking about the value difference between dollars.

What this is talking about is that the bank in question has a certain amount of value in dollars that can be transferred. While money used to be a physical item, it's not anymore, well with a majority of money that there is. Most money is digital because it allows for inflation and deflation of a currency by those who make that money.

This actually makes the value of that money much easier to control

rather than relying on physical items, but banks still make transfers with

physical items.

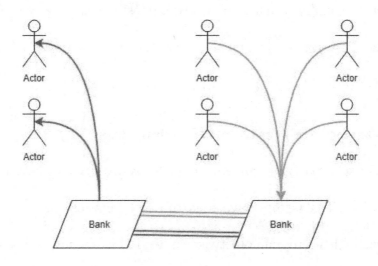

Usually, at the end of the week, there is a security truck that

transfers the amount of money that has been transferred out of that bank

going to a depository that will then disperse this money amongst the

banks who have claims to it. The bank that sent out the money will also

get its own version of a security truck holding money for money that

was transferred to that bank. Physical, paper money is still in circulation because of the system as it represents a permanency with the money. You can't copy and paste a dollar bill… well, easily that is.

The Double Spending Riddle

Digital transfers have actually been around for much longer as a concept than they have been in practice. This is because digital currency is a very easy and international way of purchasing items. There was just one problem with doing everything on the computer and that was because of an incredible invention that most of us use in our daily, if not weekly, lives; copy and paste.

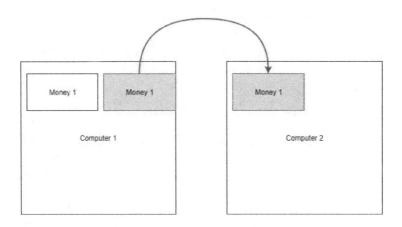

When you made a transfer of digital money, how would you go about preventing the ability to copy and paste that money just so you could have a hundred more like it? This was known as the double spending problem. In the beginning of computing history there was virtually no way of preventing the double spending problem and it is only through the internet and encryption that we can truly make our way past this problem, for a temporary amount of time.

Banks Are Prone to Double Spending, You Just Don't Know

As I noted earlier, you can do a form of copy and paste with Fiat money. Money is just an imaginary thing in that the dollar bill in your hand represents a value everyone created and doesn't actually have a measurable material value beyond the cost it took to make it. Essentially, everybody in society said that this dollar is worth this amount.

Therefore, if you can make something that looks identical to this then you have a double spending problem; it's just not digital. We often refer to this as fraud as it is a term used for trying to lie about something, which means it could be money fraud, wire fraud, or bank fraud amongst the many other types of frauds. Knowing that money could be copied and pasted, those that printed the money took steps to ensure that doing so was incredibly difficult. This is why you have things like special color ink, ridges around the edges, and custom fonts on pieces of cloth as this makes it difficult to copy it unless you have the original printer. Essentially, the first monetary form of encryption.

How to Prevent Double Spending?

Everyone Keeps Track of Everyone

Now, the first thing about the double spending problem was that they needed a way to ensure that double spending couldn't happen between two parties. Let's say that you decide to make a contract with a company for certain amount of money and then you make a contract, again, with that same company. They are the exact same contract; the only difference is that you get paid twice as much for the same amount of time. How does the company protect itself from contract fraud in this case?

There is actually a position for this and it's known as a notary. A notary has the job of being physically present at the time of signing a contract so that they can say they witnessed this contract happen and then the second contract is invalidated if that notary is not there to sign for the company. Therefore, if you manage to trick a second employee to sign a contract with you, the notary who was there for the first contract signing will know that this second contract is attempted contract fraud. This is essentially how you prevent double spending and we'll get into the details later on.

Worker ID

Now, most systems that keep track of contract invoices will usually have a form of identification. Work at a place long enough and they will give you your own specific workers identification number and this is simply to identify you as the person who you say you are. You often see this in security card keys that are way too vulnerable for most businesses.

sa064t1aMPjmBs2Cd2v-
m69YbFmMvpfNt9kt6qC3PF0l8eSV5nof5Yn2hCmS

A cryptocurrency coin has a form of this and this is often known as the worker ID (seen above). The worker ID is often a combination of

16

your specific ID attached to a randomized number that represents your worker on the computer that got the money for you. When you make the transaction, the portion of the worker ID that represents you is actually switched out with the worker ID part that represents the person you're transferring too. This is how identification of coin holders happen.

Coin ID

sa064t1aMPjmBs2Cd2v-
m69YbFmMvpfNt9kt6qC3PF018eSV5nof5Yn2hCmS

Identifications of coins is a little bit different because the identification number or stream is actually given to you by the algorithm that runs the entire system. This is a mostly randomized stream of letters and numbers partly because there are already coins in the system and those coins clash if there was an identical coin with the same stream. The only difference is that the algorithm that creates this also utilizes techniques so that the coins cannot be created in a linear order but rather an order that matches the function of the algorithm.

Therefore, when you get a coin it is a combination of randomized letters and numbers as well as a sequential combination of those in alignment with the algorithmic function designed to further randomize the coin but in a randomization pattern that can be reversed. This is how coin identification numbers are created so that no two coins have the same identification number attached to them and no one can figure out the next coin and just create the coin on their desktop.

The System Isn't Complete

The system itself is not very complete and this is why you have so many versions of cryptocurrencies out on the market because there's always someone that either wants the same amount of success they saw out of Bitcoin or someone thinks they've got a better idea for a cryptocurrency. Every year there is an improvement on the technology that exists in this market simply because it is profitable for it to do so.

Not only that, but the system is also still very vulnerable, and this isn't necessarily because of the mechanisms in place used to identify coins and workers. The vulnerability of the system is a two-part problem dealing with encryption and a difference of ideas. Encryption is used at nearly every level until you get to the point where you can earn the coin in the methodology of how that coin is earned.

Encryption is Needed for This to Work

Anyone Can Transfer the Number 1

The primary problem with the double spending problem was the fact that it could be copied and pasted. The easiest way to solve this problem is to simply make it so that it is almost impossible to copy and paste it. You can still copy and paste a blockchain node but, due to encryption, even if you were trying to use it would invalidate the use beyond a single transaction.

Cryptocurrency is not tied to the device but, rather, tied to the encryption of the coin. The encryption algorithm is unknown to anybody that is not the creator of the blockchain. This means that all that needs to happen is the blockchain needs to verify the previously recorded encryption set for both the worker ID and the coin ID. If these are the same, then what happens is that when you transfer the coin the worker ID is changed to the new identified worker. This ID is attached to a wallet and the wallet contains the worker ID that is stamped on every coin that goes into that wallet.

This means that if a person is using a cryptocurrency coin in their wallet and that coin was forcibly placed in their wallet, the blockchain would compare the worker ID to the wallet ID and deny the transaction because they didn't match. This means that if you try to have a fake coin attached to your wallet ID, the same transaction validation will occur. The coin ID will be compared to what is in the blockchain and the worker ID will be compared to the worker ID that's in the blockchain and when the blockchain sees that the worker ID attached to your coin does not match the worker ID in the blockchain, it will deny that transaction.

Breaking and Gaming the System

The problem with this is that encryption is not infallible. As an IT security specialist often says, security is not an impregnable defense but rather a delay tactic. Most blockchains will use an encryption method that will take years to break unless they know the specific passphrase needed to translate the letters.

This brings up the issue of vulnerability because what happens if the person who made it is trapped and forced to give their own passphrase? Normally, the best security against this is a rotating password that is based on a randomization method so that not even the creator will know what the passphrase is without giving himself or herself direct access.

How the Ledger Works

Everyone Sees A Transaction

The first thing to know about why this blockchain is so secure is that everyone that participates in the blockchain has a copy of the ledger. Everyone in the network can see a transaction but because it would be costly to make potentially billions of transactions every second over a network, a random group is chosen to compare the transaction to other ledgers.

21

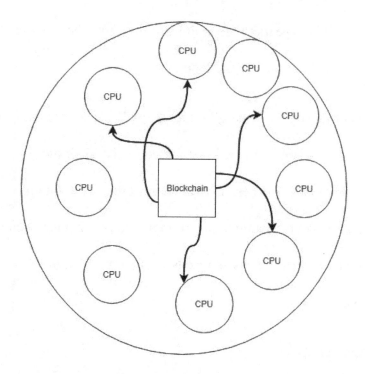

The network chooses currently participating devices to borrow their portion of the ledger so that a transaction can be compared against it.

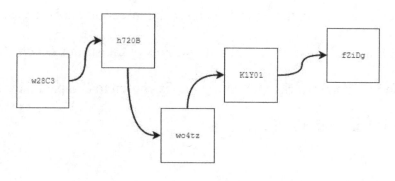

Every time a transaction is recorded, it becomes a block in the chain and thus you are able to quickly search for a transaction that happened with a specific coin.

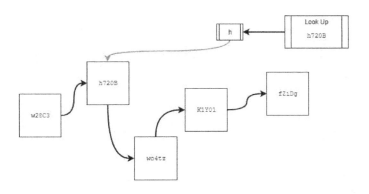

This makes the search algorithm extremely fast and then also makes it so that the comparisons can also happen at a very fast rate. Having the choices randomized increases the likelihood that no one will be able to tamper with the ledgers so that a transaction can pass, which further decreases the likelihood of fraud.

Transfers Are Verified with Ledger Comparison

Everyone on the network has their own version of the ledger making all of the ledgers original. When a transaction occurs, an update is sent to all the devices connected to the network so that everybody has

the same ledger even though everybody has an original ledger.

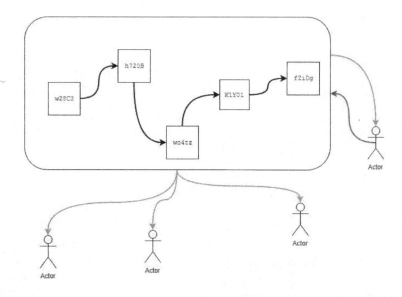

This is so that everyone can become a target for verification. 5

to 20 people on the network are chosen to see if the coin belongs to the

person trying to trade it and to see if that coin has ever been traded to

that person by the network of the cryptocurrency or by anyone else in

the system that eventually got it from the network. Based on the

percentage, the network decides whether a transaction will go through

or not.

It Usually Has A 100% Threshold

Most networks will have a 100% threshold before finally approving a certain transaction. There are some optimistic networks that allow transactions that happen at a lower threshold, but most networks try to use 100% thresholds to prevent this fraud.

The worker ID is checked to see if that worker ID has ever been on the network and is also known as *your address*, the coin is checked to see if it was ever issued by the network, and then the coin ID is compared with any worker ID that had made a transaction in the past to see if it connects to the worker ID that's making a transaction.

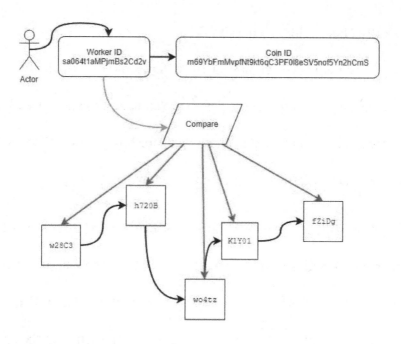

This is actually essential for understanding what blocks are in the blockchain. The most basic of blocks are simply a date of transaction, a date of verification, worker ID and a coin ID. This is also important to understanding the efficiency of the blockchain.

Blocks are Used for Small Comparisons

That was needed to understand the efficiency of the blockchain because if it wasn't built like this, it would take forever to make transactions. Millions of people interact with the blockchain which means that if you built a blockchain to simply look through all the available records it would have to go through millions of records, really a likelihood of sextillion of records at this point, before it ever reached the record you were trying to compare two.

Instead, you have a hierarchy system. Perhaps the first element would be the worker ID itself because it is the smallest number that you have.

sa064t1aMPjmBs2Cd2v

Then you have the coin ID, which is not as small as the worker ID but it's still pretty small.

m69YbFmMvpfNt9kt6qC3PF0l8eSV5nof5Yn2hCmS

By using a worker ID, they can issue numbers in a linear pattern and this allows for the binary search.

```ruby
require 'benchmark'
number = 10004

def binary_search(number)
  blockchain = (1..1000000).to_a
  binary_term_right = blockchain.length
  binary_term_middle = blockchain.length / 2
  binary_term_left = 0
  guess = true
  passes = 0
  loop do

    binary_term_middle = binary_term_left + (binary_term_right - binary_term_left)/2

    if blockchain[binary_term_middle] == number
      break
    elsif blockchain[binary_term_middle] < number
      binary_term_left = binary_term_middle + 1
    else
      binary_term_right = binary_term_middle - 1
    end

    if passes > 70
      break
    end
    passes += 1
  end
  puts "This took #{passes} passes."
end

Benchmark.bmbm do |x|
  x.report { binary_search(number) }
end
```

A binary search will almost always take several low loops.

```
Rehearsal --------------------------------------
 This took 19 passes.
   0.047000   0.000000   0.047000 (  0.056323)
------------------------------- total: 0.047000sec
```

While the algorithm above uses an integer, we cannot know how

the developer chooses to convert letters into numbers as this may be a

part of the conversion, so they may even use ASCII numbers, which

would be easy but not secure. This means that the hierarchical search

pattern only needs to go through a ledger seven times to find a worker

28

ID. Then, since there's a very small number of coins associated with most worker IDs you can just run a standard loop. The difference between this way of searching and the previous way of searching is that you are skipping trillions of instructions every second. This is why the blockchain is in nodes rather than a linear structure because it allows coins to be attached to worker IDs in the lookup system and the strings only need to be compared for their real value with very basic calculations on top of that to determine the validity of the date. This is how the blockchain works.

How It Spreads

Rarity Equals Value

The problem with this technology is that you have to spread it first and while this book will flip back and forth between cryptocurrency and blockchain, there needs to be an understanding that for a very long time blockchain was solely used for cryptocurrency and this was/is how it was/is spread.

In the beginning, Bitcoin was worthless and it was the equivalent of the fake money you see in games used for microtransactions. Essentially, Bitcoin was given away for free but eventually, people had to mine for Bitcoin and they could no longer get it for free. They had to participate in the transactions of Bitcoin to further their amount of Bitcoin, which drove up the minimum requirement of work to get Bitcoin and thus the value began.

Competitiveness Drives Rarity

By creating a system that allows people to earn money by facilitating transactions between users, you create an economy that profits off itself. By setting a finite amount of coins that can be earned you also increase the rarity of those coins.

By creating a system for people to earn money you invite competitiveness to earn more money. This has resulted in the insane value of Bitcoin and why it dropped so drastically once other cryptocurrencies started to gain a foothold in the market. Bitcoin, itself, is actually really unstable because it's imaginary money and it only has value to those who give it value.

Therefore, when the complex equations get so difficult that almost no one can mine them, and no one can really make money off of them anymore, the value drops. It was predicted in the very beginning that this would happen, but a lot of people tend to not listen to warnings as shown by the many customer support help desks that come with almost every company. Knowing this, people began to look at the intrinsic value of Bitcoin because even though it may lose its value, its technology was like nothing we had ever seen before. However, cryptocurrency as a category will always be worth something now that it exists and here's why.

This is How Fiat Currency Works

Cryptocurrency is similar to Fiat money except that Fiat money usually has a physical item representing it such as the US dollar bill. The value on that US dollar bill is imaginary and it is only ever worth the number we prescribed to it. Therefore, in reality, we could look at a

US dollar bill and say that it was worth $100 in our store while a $100 bill was worth $1. Now, there are some rules to protect against this. However, if those rules didn't exist and we chose not to follow any new rules then we could very well say this was the reality of the dollar bill versus the hundred-dollar bill even though it makes no sense because 100 is supposed to be more than 1.

However, that is how Fiat money works. There used to be something known as the golden standard and this was a time when the dollar was not just a numerical amount but exact representation of gold contained by the US Treasury. This gold standard used to be how many countries traded items in the past and now money is just an imaginary number attached to a piece of clothing that people call paper that represents the amount of work that you did to get that money. Cryptocurrency is the same thing except it's purely digital and that's it. Cryptocurrency has security implications and money has its own security implications such a special ink and unique font types. Just like cryptocurrency, money also has a chain of verification attached to it and it's usually performed by people who have the tools to verify that you are trading a U.S. dollar. This was caused by the dollars own double spending problem because there's nothing to say that you couldn't just have a printer copy and paste the dollar bill. Therefore, cryptocurrency will always have a value because it is a form of Fiat money and there is an economic society that supports it.

Cryptocurrency Only Works with the Internet

However, the one huge flaw with cryptocurrency is the requirement that you need the Internet for it to even work. You need the internet to obtain the cryptocurrency, you need it to trade it, and you need it to provide validation services. This is the one huge difference between money and cryptocurrency because money can be printed offline and you don't actually need the Internet. It means that if ever there comes a time where cryptocurrency represents the GDP of a country, the internet of that country will become the critical infrastructure that supports that country's economy.

Cryptomining Is A Collection of Methods

Proof of Work Methodology

The most common way that the blockchain was spread on the internet was with a concept known as proof of work. People would allow their GPUs to work on some algorithmic problem generated by the blockchain itself and when those problems were solved then it represented a valid transaction. By solving these problems, people would earn a percentage of the transaction that occurred as a reward for doing the work. Solving the algorithm in producing the correct answer would serve as the proof of work having been done and thus the proof of work concept was both born and named.

Bitcoin primarily is responsible for making this optional method of obtaining cryptocurrency the most popular on the market. At first, it wasn't that difficult to do this type of algebraic quick solving and so a lot of people experienced a very low bar entry into the game. This is actually what happens when someone says they're mining for currency, they are using their computing power to solve algorithmic problems.

CPU Mining

Now that you know this, it was quite obvious that CPUs would be the first that took the brunt of the calculations. This reasonably set the bar to the highest amount of computing power that a CPU could output and so, really, it generally set crypto miners apart from regular people who bought computer components.

The obvious choice was to use server cores as the number of cores gave you more options to multi-thread and solve more problems. You could generally make quite a bit of money off of this. The only problem is that even the power of CPUs wasn't quite capable of getting and succeeding above others who had already been earning money. In other words, no matter how powerful the CPU was there was a bottom line for how much you could make and everyone joining that market made everyone else in the market lose money. The calculations themselves were rather simple, it was just a matter of complexity that the blockchain had chosen beforehand that was the problem. There wasn't an efficient way of breaking down the problem into smaller chunks until there was.

GPU Mining (Graphics Processing Unit)

Lo and behold the world of crypto mining entered the GPU market thanks to a handful of programmers. You see, these programmers had found a way to allow GPUs to make the primary calculations for the algorithm and the GPU market had a lot of potential in it. Essentially, the graphical processor unit was responsible for producing the visual aspects of a computer. Almost all motherboards come with a graphical processor unit by default, but graphics cards are far more powerful and even integrated graphics are more powerful than the small graphical chips that provide motherboard BIOS interface. Instead of having 32 or 64 cores working on an algorithmic problem, you could have somewhere around 1000 to 2000 cuda cores working on that same problem. This was an exponential leap in crypto mining and it allowed a lot of people to gain a lot of Bitcoin really fast before everyone figured out what they were doing.

Now, the Bitcoin game is nearly at its end and very few people are left mining the cryptocurrency that is Bitcoin. The reason why is because of a couple factors. You have GPUs only being able to earn so

36

much and only being able to run at a certain wattage, so you have a set amount of money you can really make. Recently, bigger companies have started entering the crypto game. Competing with giant farms with thousands of cryptocurrency mining cards is not really viable for the average person. Mix this with trying to buy computer components on the market. For a good year, gamers and PC enthusiasts as well as companies who regularly update their computers had to fork out tons of money just to upgrade their GPU. As of writing this book, now that Bitcoin has drastically dropped in value, the mining cards are flooding the market and overtaking the general sales of brand-new graphics cards. This is because these crypto mining farms are often selling to make a little bit of profit back for their investment. Many people have succumbed to buying a mining graphics card only to find out that the graphics card underperforms because the mining farm changed the default settings on the device to make it more compatible with mining. Essentially, the proof-of-work concept had finally worked itself to death.

With Each Coin Comes A Different Type of Blockchain Sort Of

The BlockChain could Only Be Used for BitCoin

In the beginning, the blockchain didn't really have a purpose outside of Bitcoin primarily because the original creator only thought of the blockchain as it related to Bitcoin. This is a common thing that happens with anyone working on a project and it happened to the creator of Bitcoin. The creator of Bitcoin was so focused on developing a cryptocurrency that worked and fixed many of the problems of the past. They weren't exactly focused on creating a revolutionary technology that could change nearly all industries.

It took a very long time for even programmers to get used to the concept of the blockchain and even longer for cryptocurrency to evolve. As explained, cryptocurrency mining usually happened on the CPU at the very beginning. This is because no one really knew of a way that the complex calculations of the algorithm could be performed on the GPU. After a few updates of Bitcoin, more people began to understand it and higher people in the chain of technology began to understand what the crypto-currency market was capable of. They had the experience with developing GPUs. They also had the analytical skills to mine cryptocurrency by tricking the GPU into working together like a CPU.

Understanding the Blockchain Caused Comparisons

Once the technology got out into the market, people slowly digested what the blockchain was and this allowed people to begin to compare the blockchain to other items that might be useful. In other words, the blockchain wasn't useful at first until people started thinking about situations in which having a way to verify information was ideal in a decentralized manner.

While a blockchain could serve as a form of identification, that information also had to be able to either change or be replaced and so the idea of something like smart contracts came to exist. With a smart contract, you're able to set the properties of the contract and then if you need to change them or modify them you can access that contract, make changes, and put it back. The only difference is that when you put it back, it's now at the end of the blockchain. So, the changes to the contract are recorded in the blockchain. While the technology is not

100% perfect, it is significantly better than the current technology that we have.

The Smart Contract Was Born

Once people could realize that you could use a blockchain to store information, they wanted to make a way that allowed you to store information inside of a cryptocurrency coin. They would take an old idea and the security of that old idea and repurpose it so that it is very quick to market with possible changes in the future.

There were plenty of alternative cryptocurrencies on the market because whenever you have a successful product, you will tend to have competitors that want to capitalize on the money that's being made in that situation. The reason why smart contracts are different is because it was on top of a new cryptocurrency. It still used a very similar blockchain to previous cryptocurrency while also adding functionality to it.

Most of this technology is tied to the cryptocurrency that was invented for it because in the cryptocurrency world, the most common way you can spread the new technology is by having people invest in that technology. Thus, once Etherium came out on to the market, that was when the smart contract was really born.

The Smart Contract Wasn't Directly Connected

Building your cryptocurrency off of previous models and adding functionality to it presents a unique challenge of itself because the blockchain wasn't it really supposed to be interacted with. The fact that the blockchain wasn't supposed to be interacted with was the primary security feature of the blockchain itself so how do you go about making a non-interactable object blockchain-compatible?

The concept of the smart contract is rather confusing to most people because they're very used to understanding the blockchain. You can't actually touch the blockchain because the machine itself touches it. Knowing this, it is difficult to understand how you go about creating a smart contract, but a smart contract is really an extended coin.

Let's talk about internet packets because it's actually very easy to understand a smart contract once you understand internet packets.

41

When an internet packet is created, you first have the source of the internet packet, the destination of that packet, the lifetime that packet will have on the network, and then a small chunk of information representing your content on the network and usually these packets are broken down into very small chunks with a sequence marker. A cryptocurrency coin is made up of a worker ID that represents your wallet, the coin ID and then the last part, which is the smart contract, is anything attached to that coin ID.

Therefore, when you make a smart contract you are really making a cryptocurrency coin but you are adding everything in the smart contract at the end of a coin and so you have a unique coin ID for every smart contract that there is. This is what they mean when you are not directly interacting with the blockchain itself in a smart contract because you are fulfilling the requirements to put content after what would normally be the coin ID. Sometimes the contents are the coin ID itself but usually, it's not because you want it so that the system is able to mix your content up with a coin ID so it's not easily breakable within the system. Human language has been the linchpin that destroys many encryption methods because of common letters and phrases that we use so you want to add on to the coin a little bit of string that's randomized or inside of the string to cause disruption in the encryption so that not everything is perfectly aligned. However, while that's getting off topic, the way that a smart contract works is that it adds the information at the end of the coin and represents the coin itself and so when you submit it to the blockchain you are really still submitting a cryptocurrency coin.

The Ledger is The Blockchain

Ledger is Used By Rationalizers

The terms used to describe cryptocurrency and its methodologies are confusing. They are not confusing for the reason that you think. They begin to make sense once you have a background in programming and a small amount of knowledge in Fiat money accounting. Block is actually a programming term that refers to any line of code that means more than three lines of code in order to execute. This could be two lines but usually, it's three as a minimum. This is used as a way of describing blocks of code inside of programming and then you have the inline code and that's just code that takes up a single line.

So, if you really think about it, it makes quite a bit of sense because all you really need to see it as understanding what a chain mechanism is as well as an understanding of what block means in programming. To put it bluntly, a blockchain is a chain of code blocks. This represents the ledger that many cryptocurrencies use. The reason why it's so secure is that once a block has been made in the chain, the block cannot be modified. To modify the block, you have to modify to modify every single transaction in the chain of the block.

So, basically if you hear the term ledger, we are actually talking about the blockchain.

We just went through the basics of blockchain, including its history; and how it has evolved to what it is today.

HOW BLOCKCHAIN TECHNOLOGY IS IMPLEMENTED IN FINANCE AND TECHNOLOGY

In this chapter, we're going to go through a number of different applications of blockchain in finance, technology and programming.

Blockchain Anon Systems

In the below example, we talk about how blockchain can be implemented in programming. A common problem in database programming is the ability to access elements of it through a database id. It is easy for novice programmers to implement this in a way that is confusing and inefficient; making it difficult to access elements of the database. Some programmers make it too easily accessible; and hackers can easily figure out how to get the database ids. Using blockchain in this application eliminates the need for an id; and fixes both issues of privacy and efficiency at the same time. It uses an automatically generated encryption code or hash key; which is hard to hack. Essentially, the problem of the identification method used in today's

45

databases could be done away with if the correct method of blockchain was used to store user blocks.

Instant Secure Cross Border Payments

A lot of countries deal with the problem of inter-country trade restrictions. They do this because they can monitor the money and activity associated with financial accounts in their own country. They can easily block money transfers to certain countries.

Blockchain has the ability to neutralize the government's control over who you can and cannot have transactions with. For instance, let's say that you want to trade to someone in Russia. You live in some country that is against Russia. You can then connect a blockchain to someone who is able to trade with Russia, effectively creating a three-way pattern that allows you to stay compliant with the government yet do the transaction you want to do.

Secure Identity like IOTA

All Companies Will Participate in the Internet of Things

The Internet of things used to be a concept that was laughed at a very short while ago because no one really believed that it would be happening. I think the time that I started believing that it would happen was when my toaster was connected to the internet. I could not understand for the life of me why you would need a toaster connected to the internet. The fact of the matter is that all companies will fall to the internet of things because in business, it actually makes sense. If you want to have a good example, the dash buttons that used to exist, and still do, are not really needed. But they bring in so much extra income to Amazon that it was a brilliant move.

There's just one tiny problem with connecting appliances to the internet, which is that of security because appliances have not needed regular updates for a very long time. For instance, let's say that you bought a new fridge. It has a tablet-like screen that allows you to keep track of your food, letting you know which foods are going out of stock without you forgetting where they're located in your fridge.

This would be a service that allowed you to automatically add that food type to a shopping cart that would either be sent out to you or you could go pick it up, but it would be ready for you in either case. It would be paid for and everything would have been taken care of. To me, this sounds like a fantastic invention. But the problem is that there's nothing really protecting that application from hackers. You could try to make it so that the tablet was simply a web page, but this would actually have a few of its own complications. These complications include resetting the screen every time the fridge was unplugged by the power because web browsers are usually based off of operating system architectures. So you would have to boot the operating system and have an autorun file that opened up the browser that led you to the webpage, but this comes with its own problems.

Letting someone know what type of operating system you use is a very tricky way for social and digital hackers to figure out how to get in that system. If you tell some random person that your computer runs a Windows 7 they're very likely to not really care. However, if you tell that same information to a social hacker that is looking to get

48

information off of that computer, they will then understand that you have a system they can plug a USB into and get into automatically. They will then understand your computer no longer receives its security updates and that if they really wanted to get into your computer all they would need is your email address. Then they would send you a file that you unwittingly click on while a Powershell prompt comes up in the background, which gives them backdoor access before closing.

Understanding this concept is actually key to understanding why the Internet of Things devices need to have better security around them, ones that are not as susceptible to short range attacks and interface attacks like our modern desktops are. Operating systems usually don't have to think about the attacker directly communicating with the operating system because there are APIs that the operator has to contact in order to get access to the operating system, but oftentimes these Internet of Things devices utilize Linux as it reduces the barrier needed to have control over the device. That isn't to say that Linux is bad by default, but most of them are using very lightweight operating systems so that they can minimize the amount of device resources each device needs. This means that you lose out on security as a result. Linux is an incredibly secure operating system, but these smaller systems gut out a lot of what makes Linux Linux. Credit card information could be transferred over the internet and easily swiped if an attacker found a way to force the device to switch to their internet, which is more common than you think. I won't exactly tell you how it's done but I can tell you that the usual steps are to block your internet first before starting up theirs. Something like IOTA actually provides you with security and encryption protocols that are very lightweight and can be easily shared with other devices just like it.

It's Not A Blockchain But A Blocknet

The reason why IOTA can do this is because it's not really a blockchain more like a blocknet and that is to say that information is contained within the net of blocks rather than a linear chain. This actually allows quite a few benefits to it because the blockchain is centralized but decentralized. Everyone has access to the same ledger but everyone needs to approve a transaction to the ledger in order for the ledger to be changed. This sounds a lot like a blockchain but in this instance, it's actually quite different.

With this type of technology, there is a central ledger that does not have direct access to it. Instead, you make a transaction API call to submit a transaction and this transaction is spread to every node in the network for consensus approval. This would prevent things like altering information or using a credit card where items on the credit card are not 100% accurate and similar fraud charges. All of the information going to the API is encrypted so at every user point the information is already encrypted and the API call sends out a consensus request to all devices that should respond back as soon as they get it whether they concede or refuse. Based on this, the transaction is made in the ledger and then another service can now access the blockchain or rather ledger to confirm that the information has changed and then take certain actions upon it. Therefore, it is a combination of both decentralized and centralized control for the best of two worlds because no one actually directly interacts with the ledger so no one can really tamper with it.

Meanwhile, in order to make changes on the network, everyone has to agree with those changes.

Everyone Involved is Involved

There are two unique properties here. The first property is that this type of blockchain is actually very reminiscent of the Internet of Things idea and that is that all the devices are connected in a household, but this idea expands upon it saying that all devices on the internet of things are connected to each other.

The reason why I called this the blocknet is because it's a lot like the internet. Believe it or not, HTML is a ledger of rules that every browser either agrees or disagrees to commit to. Regardless of which device you go to, most browsers will either use HTML, xHTML, and usually that's it. There are a few smaller ones out there but usually, those two are the majority of the internet with some very useful tools in the background. In order to make changes to HTML, there has to be a consensus amongst developers that changes need to be made and reasons have to be given. No one can just willy-nilly make changes to

HTML, you actually have to go through a very lengthy process by contacting nearly everyone who's in charge of HTML to see if a change can be implemented and they have to agree with you in order to even do anything about it. Yet, even though it is one ledger of digital rules, thousands of computers follow those rules and update when that ledger updates. There are some unique differences between the browsers, but it's usually quite consistent that browsers stay updated with the latest HTML trends except for whatever Microsoft makes.

The second property is that the blockchain is malleable and can be changed. Sometimes, you might need more or less information. With this type of network, you can section off what type of transactions your information needs to make, which allows multiple devices to interact with each other based on needs. If you recall, most of what happens on previous blockchains was immutable, which meant that it couldn't be changed. With a set of rules that just allows for a transaction of information to occur, you can modify the amount of information in that transaction. This IOTA is very similar to how JSON works to communicate information from the front-end to the back-end in web browsers, which is how *most* interactions happen on the internet.

Enforced Accountability

All Actions Can be Recorded and Non-Editable

A great feature that's part of QuickBooks is the fact that you cannot make edits to information without those modifications being recorded. This is because when you make those audits or editing modifications, you are essentially changing tax records and so all modifications are recorded for the purpose of proving something happened at some date. This makes QuickBooks a lot better than Excel for taxes.

The problem is that there's not much software outside of the tax world that generally holds people accountable. The closest thing that we have to it that is very common in society, is the customer support ticket. With a customer support ticket, the support ticket is assigned to a team and then someone from the team begins to interact with the customer and everything is recorded to that customer support ticket. This provides a way for the company to go back and review the material as well as hold those that dealt with the customer in the customer support ticket accountable for their own actions. The reason why companies want to do this is because sometimes customer representatives have a habit of not doing what the company wants the employee to do. For instance, a customer representative might tell a customer that the customer's problem is not worth their time and that the customer needs to be more intelligent about their decisions. Almost no company on the planet wants this. So, what happens is that the customer makes a review that's bad and at some point in time in the future, the company will either go through a standard routine check of customer tickets. Or the PR around the issue will get so bad that the company will find out and they'll be able to track down the individual.

However, many companies don't have a system like this for anything other than the customer representatives because it's difficult to conceptualize not only what needs to be done but how it is going to be implemented. The blockchain represents the implementation of this problem because with a blockchain you are able to ensure records are being kept of people's actions and you can begin implementing it in nearly everything because you already have an implementation standard. This type of blockchain allows for companies to hold themselves and others accountable in the market of ideas and in the court of law.

Blocks Can Be Assigned to Members

The best part is that both the customer and the employee can stay anonymous until it is absolutely necessary to require their names. The most common way to figure out a system is to look for developers that work within the system and then pay attention to the internet when that person seeks help on forms. A great majority of a developer's initial work is built on getting help from others who are more knowledgeable than they are because it is impossible to memorize everything about programming.

The problem with this is that when you're dealing with customer support tickets that have to do with the platform, you're looking at being able to attach a real-life name to the person who both is asking the question and the person giving me the answer. Social hackers

understand that certain bugs are fixed in different ways depending on

the programming language you have. A huge problem in figuring out

the weaknesses of a system involves figuring out what language that

system uses because even programming languages are subject to bugs

and problems. Therefore having real names attached to it causes of a

huge issue because when that developer begins to ask questions about

the back-end language, they are going to use the code that they're

having a problem with and this lets the social hacker understand what

programming language is used for the back end, which makes the back

end even more vulnerable.

I have said in the past, blocks in your average blockchain are

primarily made up of a timestamp, a worker ID, and a coin ID.

However, in a valuable blockchain system you can actually have it so

that instead of having a worker ID you have a random digit that

represents an employee and a random digit that represents a customer

and have two different databases for them based off of a specialized ID.

This hides both databases and the names associated with customer support, hides the name of the person submitting a question, encrypts all of the information, and creates a system of accountability.

A New Supplier Network

This new system of accountability can actually be used to create a new system of supplier networks because a great portion of the work in a supplier network is verifying that something has arrived, and something has left. It is very difficult to build a system that will stand the test of time that ensures that something will arrive, and something will depart. For example, let's say that we own a packing company the allows you to send various parts out. Normally, the person who makes the part can only ever put a modification on the part and this is a problem because the part manufacturer has to rely on the carrier to verify that something has been delivered. This can lead to lost packages and frustration in some cases.

In the Internet of Things, most things are online. The best part about using a blockchain is that you can attach a GPS to it by putting a GPS unit in your box that will transmit the location of the device. It is also transmitted in a format that is very secure. You don't want to willy-nilly give someone else's address away. This is the primary reason why part manufacturers do not put a sticker on the side of the box is because it doesn't transmit the data and it doesn't allow for secure information to be shared over the internet.

Recruitment Reference Checks BEGONE!

As I've mentioned many times in the past, the primary problem that we deal with in middlemen is that most of it is dedicated to simply verifying if the information is true. The reason why this is difficult to do is that you have to have systems that people can trust before people will trust that information. Naturally, if you have a driver's license then the most common thing that the person will trust is the maker of that driver's license. So what you really have is a government that makes the driver's license and the place you're using the driver's license with wants to check with the government to see if it's legitimate. This usually involves a very small fee for the work that's involved with checking that driver's license.

59

One of the problems that could significantly be a benefit to people utilizing the blockchain is the idea of secure references. A big problem with references is that you tend to have to trust people on both ends of the system whether it be the person who's applying for the job or the person that was actually listed as a reference, both of which could be lying. This is an enormous problem for security positions in areas where you generally want to make sure that neither of these two people are lying but you have situations where it's a possibility and it's actually quite difficult to catch them in that lie. This is until you incorporate blockchain technology into references because blockchains can be immutable.

Let's say that you have been working with a company for a number of years and when you first started working with the company, part of the process was submitting your name to a reference company. Essentially, this would be an employer reference found on a resume but the information about whether you worked for a company or not would be stored by a company that provides this as a service to many companies around the world. This provides verifiable proof with minimal fees that you were part of an organization because the company has to have direct access to the section of their references. This allows you to do multiple things.

First, you can have a company sets up a reference database for everyone that works at the company so that other companies can figure out the people who are lying and the people who are telling the truth. This reduces a significant amount of the work involved in running background checks and ensuring the equality of work that's going to come from a specific employee. The employee ID number can be used to provide information about the employee work history without actually having to provide confidential information (this differs based on local law).

The last thing that can be done with this is actually something that involves security for those who apply to jobs. The primary problem with resume websites is that unless the name is very well known in the PR space, you don't really know if the resume website is legitimate or not. For instance, a common scam that's going around at the point of writing this book is a job offering from a company that disguises itself as Amazon and then links you to something like AmazonInfo.org and this means that when you submit your information to this website, you now have to deal with the repercussions of being scammed. This scam website wants your credit card information to set you up with a kit that will "prepare you to work at Amazon" and then once they get your credit card information they also have your resume which usually includes your phone number and your email address so they can begin blasting you with scam calls and scam emails. This is a huge problem and there is no real way to stop it other than removing the individual and that individual will have another individual just like it pop up very shortly after or during the stopping of that individual.

Something else that you can do is have a verification of resume websites so that not only employers have trusted websites they can hire people from, but they can also provide security for the potential employees looking to obtain a job there. Instead of relying on websites that tell you that they are safe or legitimate, you can go to the well-known reference company that the website uses to verify that they are an active user with that system of references. This allows security for employers and employees while also making the life of employers and employees significantly easier.

Payments with No Middle Man

Cryptocurrency Has No Border, Et tu Blockchain

The benefit of blockchain also comes in the form of how you can connect people together because a lot of the verification systems and payment systems used today require government cooperation. The government might want to sanction a certain country based off of their actions. However, you as a company have significant dealings with that another company in that country. This causes such sanctions to practically bankrupt your company. This is not much of an issue with a lot of home-based companies that don't work internationally, but companies such as microchip manufacturers and things like that might find themselves in a pickle when the majority of microchips are made in China. Yet, your government has decided to block most of the trade coming from China. Essentially, creating a huge scarcity that's purely political when there doesn't need to be one in your company's vision.

A blockchain doesn't require government cooperation as of right now which means that you can essentially have a system that ignores the need for government if you absolutely need to. Mind you, there are border customs and different situations when you are shipping things like physical products but in the case of something like software keys or schematics, these are purely digital and most of the problem deals with having digital work done but not being able to pay for that work or being taxed on the pay for that work at a significant rate because of this political issue.

With a blockchain, you can register a customer in your accounts that stays permanent and you can apply cryptocurrency to that customer. The reason why this is important is because by being able to tie cryptocurrency, a currency not currently controlled by the vast majority of governments in the world, you are able to avoid being taxed on paying or being prevented to pay for that work. You can essentially convert your money into cryptocurrency, exchange it to the person who did the work, then that person can take the cryptocurrency to an exchange market and get the money not only from the cryptocurrency but in the currency that they prefer. There are actually systems like this in place right now, but they are really small and a lot of people don't trust them because they're usually not made within the country that they live in, therefore they are very suspect. Also, a few countries have banned the use of cryptocurrencies to prevent this; so this could be an issue as well.

In-House Cryptocurrency

This is a very unique idea because it's not really one that surfaced in the middle or even mainstream market and is still relatively small. An in-house cryptocurrency allows you to pay for things at companies using your allowance of cryptocurrency that the company provides you with. If you think of companies that incentivize work that's done fast or work that's done to a very high quality, you can think of the same system where kids are given coins for doing good jobs at their school and being able to amass a certain amount of those coins to earn prizes. This is very similar to that because the reward system is actually in use in quite a few countries except for places like The American or The European system. The reason why the reward system exists is it be encouraging workers to do more than just the bare minimum.

Workers understand that they will get paid if they do their job but many workers, when they come to realize this, tend to only do the bare minimum amount of work at their place of work because they know they'll get paid. When someone knows that there is no incentive to go above and beyond what they're actually being paid for, it is very difficult to get cooperation within the workplace and so things slow down significantly. In America, the way that they like to reward good work is through parties, company get-togethers, retreats, and every once in a while you might actually hear about a company that rewards you with a holiday present ranging anywhere from turkey to something like a cruise that you may have wanted to go on. The reason why these companies do this is because it creates a personal connection with the worker of that company but the problem with personal connections is that it causes personal problems (Of course, we are not talking about big banks here; which is a completely different story).

If a person works for a company for a decade and they have begun to think of themselves as part of the family, they will indeed work more than they need to so that everybody in the family stays happy. No one in the family likes the person who does the least amount of work because there's always something to complain about and so more and more reasons are created to get rid of that person. It creates a sense of competitiveness but in a less direct way. Companies that reward their workers with things like a new iPhone or Samsung do so based off of company goals that are directly increasing the competitiveness amongst their workers. The difference between the two is that workers that are compensated with gatherings and things that allowed them to enjoy something with other workers creates a Cooperative environment. Workers that are incentivized to do better because they will earn prizes actually creates a cutthroat environment. You see this in police dramas and shows depicting office reporters where they often try to outdo one another so that they can get more benefits than the others in the group. Those that ultimately do get those benefits are actually despised by everyone else and so it eventually evolves from being a collective group of cutthroat individuals looking for benefits into a strong brotherhood of rotational benefits. This is highly detrimental and is definitely very centered around who manages to get what.

In-house cryptocurrency is a different option than both of these because cryptocurrency by itself actually promotes the ability to exchange for money or for items. Therefore, you can think of it like a mixture between you can either choose to get a bonus paycheck or you can win the cruise prize that you might have wanted. The best part about this type of In-House cryptocurrency is the fact that different amounts of the cryptocurrency can be distributed to all workers at the same time. This also provides a level of performance checking to see who's doing the best and who's doing the worst. It's a very unique combination of performance checks, reward checks, and co-operation encouragement. You see it encourages cooperation because everyone gets rewards but the person with the lowest amount of rewards is the ultimate denominator of how much everyone gets, and it creates a weak link that encourages others to help that weak link.

Ripple: Earthport Service Payment System

What is it? It's Not a Blockchain

Ripple is a very unique type of cryptocurrency being used to provide an easier method of transactions between banks. It is something that can be invested in, but the primary use for it is for banks looking to do cross-border transactions where it would normally take a business week or longer. It was actually developed in 2012 and is recently a hot market because of the enormous value boost that occurred in 2017. Ripple is a Protocol and not a Blockchain, which means it's a set of rules for banks to use in order to make transfers *through* Ripple Network.

XRP Tokens Finality with Drops and IOU Non-finality

XRP is the name of the currency and is primarily what is used to make transactions. Ripple also makes use of something called an IOU, which is a promise that a transaction will occur eventually. IOUs are agreements between banks where one bank does not have yet enough money to make their half of the transaction, but the other bank does and the other bank agrees to the transaction, accepting the IOU that can be redeem. This creates a loan-type system that banks can use to continue making transactions, which allows the market of business to continue.

XRP, unlike IOU, has a finality to it. There are exactly 100 Billion XRP, but it's important to remember that cryptocurrency coins can be spent in the billionths or more so a transaction might be 0.0000000000000000000000000012 XRP fee, which means it's not a big issue at all.

Marketmakers: Buy and Sell Orders

The way that trades happen are through devices/people known as Marketmakers. When someone submits a request, they submit it through XRP by exchanging something like USD to a Marketmaker that will buy it with XRP. Someone else submits something like CAD to the same Marketmaker that will buy it with XRP. That Marketmaker will then buy back the USD person's XRP with CAD and then use the USD to buy back the CAD person's XRP. At some point during this transaction cycle, the Marketmaker will charge a fee of their own to make money off of the transaction. This is how Marketmakers can make money and how the Ripple Net functions for the most part for cross-border exchanges.

HOW BLOCKCHAIN TECHNOLOGY IS IMPLEMENTED IN SMART CONTRACTS

Ethereum and Smart Contracts

There are 2 Ethereums out there, Ethereum and Ethereum Classic, which is a somewhat important thing to point out. They both have Smart Contracts in them, but they are two different platforms. The reason why the difference is important has to deal with Decentralized Autonomous Organization or the DAO.

The DAO would serve as a Networked Hedge Fund, something investors could buy into if they wanted to support some organization through Ethereum. Investors would by DAO tokens and give them to Decentralized Applications or DAPPs, which allowed them to invest and get voting power like stocks do. In order to buy those tokens, investors would have to use Ether, the transactional money of Ethereum.

The problem was when investors wanted to leave this little ecosystem, they needed to use the "Split Function". This function served as a way to exit the ecosystem, get the Ether they invested back, and gave them an option to create a Child DAO that would become an Ether Investment Firm of sorts. With intelligent inventions often comes intelligent exploiters, which meant this system of leaving was exploitable as the DAO had to be computed. A hacker made a recursive Split Function, which caused a continuous release of Ether until ⅓ of DAO funds were released into their pockets.

This massive issue stole a lot of Ether, affecting both DAO and ETC (Ethereum Classic) communities until the ultimate decision was made to split those communities. ETH (Ethereum) serves as a new cryptocurrency with a blockchain that prevents this while ETC allowed those who had amassed Ether to continue operating. With a new coin on the market, Ethereum was created and the community that had left managed to get the funds back.

With Ethereum Came Smart Contracts

ETC became just another cryptocurrency while ETH became a cryptosoftware company with a mutable blockchain. While the fast majority of the community feels that the blockchain is immutable, it can be changed by those who hold power over it and this was needed in order to get the money back. By making it mutable, it also made it open to certain changes like the ones we're talking about now.

ETH, unlike ETC, is backed by what's known as the Ethereum Alliance which is comprised of some very high value firms like Microsoft and JP Morgan. This means they have a lot of weight that can be thrown around, and ETH is now worth almost 15x ETC.

What is a Smart Contract?

Proof of Stake

As mentioned before, cryptocurrency makers wanted to do a better job at making less of an impact on computer power so now there's something called Proof of Stake. The way that this process works is that instead of creating a difficult problem for people to solve, rewards are handed out to random people on the network based on the stake they have in the network.

The reason why this switch took place is that it is far less prone to a takeover and less resources are used to maintain the network. Essentially, all you have to have in order to make Ether in Ethereum is Ether itself. The more of it you have, the more likely you are to make money off of it. Bitcoin had a takeover with mining farms, which could horde all of the earning because a single computer couldn't compete with something like that. As a result, the cryptocurrency has an active market where everyone tries to get a bigger stake in the network.

Additionally, if you tried to tamper with the network or the transaction then you risk having all of your Ether taken away from you or the reward. This would be automatically decided by the Blockchain when it detected tampering.

It's Still a Blockchain Sort Of

It's important to understand that a Smart Contract is still a coin, it's just that the coin has the contractual state inside of it. Smart

75

Contracts are rather interesting because it is a saved Code State Listener. To understand what a Code State Listener is, you have to understand the difference between Parallel and Linear Processing. In computing, everything happens in a linear processing pattern, which means everything goes from Point A to Point B.

Having said that, Parallel Processing is where Linear Processing happens at the same time so while you go from Point A to Point B, someone else goes from Point C to Point D. Now, a Code State Listener is when a Third Person is waiting on both of you to arrive at the same time in order to begin. This is how Parallel Computation is done.

In a Smart Contract, there's a bit of code that waits for Conditions to be met before running a completion or at-end-of-program code block. Therefore, a Smart Contract waits until you do what you need to before it begins running.

The way the blockchain works in this system is that *it* is the one that enforces that the contract is followed. Therefore, someone creates a Smart Contract, that Smart Contract "listens" for your conditions to be met, and when those conditions are met the blockchain executes the Smart Contract.

Smart Contracts Are Not Applicable to Everything

Conditionals Are Binary

One of the problems with a Smart Contract is that it needs to be an either-or choice, it cannot be multi-conditional. For instance, let's say that you have the option to rent a car or buy a car. If you rent the car, the Smart Contract has been fulfilled according to the blockchain and no more will be demanded. Essentially, they will have to have a new Smart Contract for months on end until the company sees it as paid.

Smart Contracts cannot have Recurring Events, which means something like renting requires new contracts with new signatures.

Conditionals Have to Be Binary

Conditions also have to be quantifiable in a "Did" or "Did not" manner, which means partial pay is not an option. Let's say that a consumer wants to pay for a specific Service and that Service is tied to a Smart Contract. The Service may cost 300ETH and thus, unless 300ETH is paid to a specific account, the contract is still live. However, the consumer offers to pay for a product that your team needs like a new editing software and wants to compensate the cost by modifying the contract. This cannot be done and while there are ways around it, it still represents a limitation of Smart Contracts.

Listener Overload

This has not happened yet, and I am surprised that no one has figured this out, but there's a potential for a listener overload. Each time a Smart Contract is made, it has to listen and that means code is running in the background to make this possible. Thus, you can recursively open listeners with small contract loads and you would need a *ton* of ETH, but it is a vulnerability of the system. What I think would happen is that the entire system would become incredibly slow to the point where some might find it unusable. Beyond these things, Smart Contracts are applicable to a lot of situations and that makes them incredibly useful.

THE FUTURE OF BLOCKCHAIN IN MARKETING AND SALES

Universal ID Distribution

Non-User Based Tracking

Most of the issue is often about gaining new customers and, as we've seen with the Mark Zuckerburg conference, a lot of people don't like thinking that their personal information is tracked when they're not a user and didn't sign anything. The beauty about this is that Blockchains can ensure their information is secured and they can be assigned a Blockchain number instead of trying to identify who the user is.

A lot of personal information goes into "shadow profiles" and many of them simply record the type of websites you go to because keylogging is illegal. They also record your mouse as you visit their website so as to see if their designs are luring people in. This is data that is ultimately disposed of at the end of the month as it is difficult to

79

maintain storage around this, but those that are not tech-savvy don't have a method of being sure. However, if those people understand that their information is held in a blockchain, is completely anonymized, and the entire blockchain is thrown away and recreated, such fears might go away.

Success and Fail Profiles

Attached to the concept of anonymization are Success and Fail profiles, which refers to when a user clicks on the call-to-action or they do not. The sad thing is that most websites have to tie this to some identifying marker, with the easiest one being the IP address that comes in on the marker. However, if everyone shares data then this becomes an issue of targeting people at their devices, the primary reason why VPNs have shot up in use. Knowing this, the Blockchain produces a very interesting opportunity because recording IP addresses is no longer viable at this point, but a Blockchain ID is still usable. Essentially, it'd be nothing more than a Javascript cookie that collects information, much like what is used today but this information would be based on randomized ID rather than the IP address that connects to the server.

80

Then you could create anonymous associations like the language used or the currency used, which are detectable default settings. It provides a far more targeted way of tracking without actually know who the person is based on a cookie that you dropped in. This allows you to create these profiles to a much more accurate degree without sacrificing privacy.

Advertisement Auditing

Showed Versus Clicked

One of the most expensive things in advertising is just proving that the advertisement has actually been effective in causing an action from the user. With all online advertisement methods, there comes a point where the advertisement either results in a click or not a click. This would seem like a relatively uncomplicated problem, but the problem comes in the form of companies that get paid by those advertisements.

Let's look at the Google advertisement program because this is a program where you can obtain a key associated with your account that

81

allows you to get money for advertising inside of your product. Websites and applications both use this form of advertisement interaction because it's really easy to implement but it is really easy to fake as well. One of the most notorious problems with online advertisements is the determination of real clicks vs. fake clicks because fake clicks are caused by companies who want to earn money from ad revenue without having a lot of customers. Essentially, the old way of doing this was to set up a web browser on a computer and continuously reload that computer and click on an advertisement only to shortly thereafter close the link that the click led to. Now, this is a lot less common than it used to be because it's quite easy to figure out whether an advertisement is being clicked on because the company wants to make money from it or the customer is actually engaged with the advertisement itself.

The way that companies stopped, mostly, fake clicks in this form was to tie the click to an address but this just elevates the problem to a more complex problem. You see, you have things like VPNs that allow users to change IP addresses so that even though you detected a click happened just five seconds earlier, it looks like it's coming from a different address the next time that the click happens. The reason why this is difficult to detect is because you have to either assume that it is a different click, or you have to find the MAC address to the device that's doing the clicking.

Web browsers have naturally been able to implement this, and the fake clicks are usually people who get paid to click, but that's also really difficult to track. Facebook is notorious at this point for having these fake clicks because you might see thousands of people clicking on an advertisement but the only way that you know that they're fake is if all the clicking comes from a country that has a low GDP. Even then, it's speculation and not fact at that point because you can't exactly prove that it's a fake click yet plenty of people do this. Again, companies have tried to combat this by making it illegal inside of the terms of service to do such a thing but it's really difficult to track.

However, with the blockchain you can track it. With the blockchain you can tie known addresses to previous users in a very small format. You can actually do this with users now in a basic spreadsheet, but the complexity comes from how you go about verifying fake vs. real clicks. For instance, a good majority of how fake clicks are detected today are usually associated with the behaviors of the person doing the clicking and this is why Google gets paid a lot for their advertisements.

With a blockchain, you can access several points of data that might normally have been off-limits to you before. For example, in the regular world you do not have immediate access to the GDP of a country at the same time you have access to the MAC address of the computer that's clicking on it in the same spreadsheet but with a blockchain you can tie the current GDP with the current MAC address and begin following that Mac address to see what the computer does as it relates to your advertisements and how often those clicks are made.

Further information can be given at that point such as how much that person makes according to their reported amount on another blockchain, where that person lives, perhaps what that person does on an Android phone, and the information goes further and further and further because people trust security-based Systems. Therefore, things that have previously been off-limits such as a person's address as it relates to the advertisement can now be made available to the Advertiser because that Advertiser is a trusted member that isn't going to use the address for bad things. Because you cannot tamper with the information, blockchains provide a way of accessing encrypted information, because those that access the blockchain have to be pre-approved, and because companies tend to work together, you have a situation where you can now track the behavior patterns and verify the existence of people in countries that you would normally not have those rights in.

Having 100 cell phones connected to the same IP address with all different Mac addresses can be simulated but knowing that they're connected to the same IP address and knowing that that IP address has been consistently flagged in the blockchain as used for fake purposes creates a verified way of ensuring the difference between fake clicks and real clicks. Such a process saves millions of advertising dollars.

Company and Product Authenticity

Anyone Can Use A Bar Code

The truth of the matter is that pretty much anybody that has a printer can create barcodes of their own. This is true of trademarks and logos but with the blockchain, it becomes a different ideal altogether. It's been a very long time since the standard barcode has been updated and the problem is that these markers on these boxes are used to identify organizations. For instance, you will commonly see the FCC logo and the FTC logo on electronical products depending on their uses. You will often see certification logos on the sides of desktops to certify that the product is working as expected. However, these logos can be duplicated because all you need to have is an image of that logo.

Photoshop is a fantastic tool but there's one problem and that it is able to create anything from a photo. This means that Chinese (which is a country that's most notorious for this) manufacturers that are not legitimate can take the FCC Logo and put it on the back of any technology that would require it. This allows them to trick users into believing that the item has been checked by the FCC and it is an aspect of the used product market that many IT professionals have spoken about. This brings us to the next topic though.

Branding With Special Font Encryption

When you deal with barcodes, you are creating an item for scanning and the newest form of barcode is actually known as a QR code. Those little weird boxes that provide additional information with them. You need a QR reader in order to translate them, but they do give extra material on top of what would normally classified as a barcode. With blockchain technology, this becomes a different story because now you can have a logo that has unique ink that only shows up in a phone. All you need to do is scan with your phone and this can legitimize a product or delegitimize it. Essentially, you can have as much encryption as a dollar bill on your own branding that a customer can then scan to access information on a secure server that verifies that this is a branded product.

The reason why this hasn't been doable in the past is because smartphones have notoriously not had the best of cameras, there was no way to secure the code in a way that copyright infringers couldn't copy, and there wasn't a way to secure that information so that it couldn't be tampered with. That last one is very important because when you let people know where the information is, bad actors will try to find out how to get access to that information. If the information is part of a blockchain, you can now modulate access to different verification blocks. Therefore, only your company can transverse the blockchain itself while the customer sees a block in the chain, effectively isolating it from the rest of the chain. Plus, the scan material itself can be an identification marker such as a certain combo of red and green might pick up Starbucks or Chugg, which would then cause a lookup in their database that no one else can access.

Products Can Tell A Story

One of the unique traits of an item like this is that each product can tell a story. Unlike the Barcode or the QR code, a lot more information can be tied to a block. This allows a story of the product to be contained within the scan, such as where the materials came from, what went into the product, and a lot more. This creates a personal connection between the company and the potential consumer.

Anonymized Marketing

Personal Ads Without Being Personal

Since the advertisement information isn't personal information, one no longer needs to risk an incident like the "gay caught at work". Instead, each advertisement is tied to a blockchain profile and that profile can then have safe and unsafe advertisements. Therefore, if Lucy the lesbian opens up her browser at work, this identification number is not the one she has at home and so only safe advertisements show up at work. Additionally, work environments can specify what type of advertisements they want through this system, such as adverts targeting based on sex appeal or "LGBT" items, which can cause controversy amongst those that pass by and those that wanted to keep that information private.

Ads Fit the Audience and Sometimes the Person

In addition to this, adverts that are hosted through a blockchain can meet audience needs rather than an individual person. One of the most annoying things about adverts is when you get them for totally unrelated items. For instance, one video that might be talking about HTTP 2.0 has an advert off to the side that's talking about the new Furby or this excellent gaming website.

Based on Blockchain information, this blockchain id can be tied to what adverts were successful and which ones were not. So, if a tech advert is more successful for this person, Furby electronics and a game won't show up. However, if that person is interested in tech but has shown to have clicked on game adverts then the game advert could show up but the Furby electronic would never come up. This speaks to the tech audience, not to the person who might be interested in games. The difference is that a tech audience is far more likely to click on an advert for server tech than they are for a game unless that specific person has done so in the past, this increases the likelihood of successful adverts.

Blockchain Profiles and Saving Money

Make Money On "Adcoins"

Adverts are not something people want to see, pretty much ever. Knowing this, a company that wanted to support creators came out that was known as Brave. The way that Brave works is that a user can put money towards people they support through micropayments. Most of the reason as to why we see advertisements is because the website wants to make money, so users help support them by themselves. If 1 million people watch an ad-free video and each of them gives over $0.01 USD, the creator can get $10,000. To give you an understanding of the difference, usually 1,000 views = $1 and so putting 1,000,000 to that you get $1,000. So, in this situation, the Brave app actually pays more, which means that adverts could be avoided altogether and make the creator even more money. Secure transactions can be handled through blockchain as Brave suggests that they do.

This system is brilliant, except for 1 issue and that is that it removes advertisements completely. Brave *also* handled this because it has a Rewards Program for those that do not mind watching adverts if it means they can be rewarded directly for doing so, which is then something that can be given to support creators. Essentially, Brave created an ecosystem that allows users to prevent websites from tracking them, rewards them for adverts they don't mind watching, blocks annoying ads, saves data, exchanges in cryptocurrency, and provides a new way of searching the internet.

Their system makes sense, but the truth is that other browsers should also be complying with this and they're not. Users are constantly submitted to watching adverts to the point that items like Adblock Pro are used just to ensure an ad-free experience. Creators hate advertisements as much as the next person, but people would rather support their favorite creators directly if they could. Possibly the worst part about the internet is the invasive ad system unless you incentivize users to it. The website gets paid to host the advertisement, users should be paid to watch it because they *don't* want to watch it.

Companies have a hard time conceptualizing why this should be the way that it is because companies think they'd have to spend more money. People know websites only use advertisements because it supports them as a website. Advertisers waste a *ton* of money on ad campaigns that target entire classes of people who could care less about the product. Even worse, most websites get paid a fraction of a penny for a view and maybe a penny for a click. Therefore, you have a system where a ton of money is being wasted because you don't know who you're advertising to *exactly* and the only information you're relying on is the tracking history of web searches and desktop applications. On the other side, websites make a decent living if they can pump out enough content so that you'll look at adverts enough times to get paid and hopefully people will sometimes click on ads, which means it's a costly wasteful gotcha system.

With a system like Brave, websites are supported directly by the userbase and often much more so because users don't know how much to give so they usually over give. Those that don't have money opt-in to an ad program that will give them money that they can then contribute using a no-border cryptocurrency that can be sold in an exchange for money. Those advertising in the ad program have access to the likes and interests of everyone they're adverting to, so they know exactly the customer they are selling to and they only ever spend as much money as they want versus a situation where they have to estimate a budget. Like Facebook gets $50 for 5,000 views with no promises of clicks or even how targeted it truly is, whereas something like Brave allows you to pay out money for every full viewing you get to someone that's extremely well-targeted.

Possible Government Compliant Ad Database

Finally, this system is non-invasive and allows users to participate in a way where there's no database of personal information just for advertisements. Advertisers don't get access to location, places visited, or other information that even the government might be jealous of because **they don't need it** as they're more interested in what type of customer, they're selling to than where they live.

This means the possibility of a complete Government Compliant Ad Database can be made, where companies can submit advertisements that can rated. Kids don't need to see porn and adults don't need to see "kiddy games", which creates an ESRB-type system for advertisements. What information can be collected can finally be regulated *by the government* and no company that's built on selling invasive information to advertisements would have to switch to a less invasive model. It would lower data costs vastly for the majority of people, protect people, de-incentivize NSA-level spying, and increase the effectiveness of advertisements while reducing targeting people individually.

No Leakable Points… Sort Of

Perhaps the best part about this sort of blockchain technology is that there are no "leakable" points. You no longer have to collect Big Data via tracking just to get the edge on marketing because people will hand you their data! Such a system opens up an entirely new world of advertising, one that focuses on getting feedback from customers without knowing who the customers are. A survey can be asked to determine company image without it being shoved inside of people's content. You can have several different ad campaigns to see which ad does best with which crowd for far less money.

This means that all of this information is passed over a secured connection to a blockchain that's encrypted and only accessible to people who are authorized, by the consumer, to have access. No more guessing, no more useless profiles, no more wasted money and advertisements mean something again.

HOW BLOCKCHAIN TECHNOLOGY IMPROVES ONLINE SAFETY

Secure Storage and Complete Encryption

Encryption with a Unique Algorithm

The beauty of encryption is that it can be carried out in a number of ways, which means that security is actually a factorial problem. So, let's say that you use SHA-256 to encrypt your stuff, which is insecure, and you shouldn't, but it's one way in which you can encrypt items, which is important. Had the method not found a way to be broken, it would take less than a day to break it.

However, what if you encrypted it with MD5 (still somewhat good)? Well, this would take about 6 months after the hacker *figured out* that they were dealing with an MD5 encryption and then take 1 day on top of that to break SHA-256. That's pretty good, but can we do better? Yes we can! We can mix MD5 with SHA-256! At this point, you're looking at a ridiculously long number that would cause you to

97

die along with 300 generations before you ever got to the point of breaking what's there. Believe it or not, that's the type of encryption that's on the blockchain.

Obscuring Data Location

Half the battle in finding sensitive information is hiding information, because when a hacker comes into your system that's what they're looking for. The way that hackers find information are through bugs, security holes, and people. This means that if you want to hide something like a blockchain, all you have to do is create as many barriers to it as you can. With a blockchain, this is quite easy because every block in the blockchain is going to be impossible to find unless you know the exact identification marker used when finding it. If you can figure this out, you are halfway to figure out how to find the others. However, once you do you then need to decrypt it and unless you know the salt (added in word to prevent repetitive patterns in encryption), good luck every doing that.

A Backups Backup

The interesting thing about a blockchain is that it can be used to backup and verify that data hasn't changed. In a company backup, there's usually a way to keep that backup secure also known as source control. This allows developers to keep a secure copy of the code on hand so that if something happens that went horribly wrong, it's as easy as copy and paste. However, backups tend to go untouched until you get to the next stable point, so they just sit there, vulnerable. A social hacker could get into the building and copy the backup for their own use, which means there needs to be a way to secure it and ensure that everyone has a backup. A Blockchain can be used to do this.

Restoration of Modifications

7 Years on Everyone's Computer

A blockchain can be timestamped so all of those tax records the IRS requires that you have for 7 years can both be automatically store in a blockchain and regularly released every 7th year. This reduces the need for bulky paperwork and ensures the security on those files, but it can also be stored on every secure company computer to give you a way of backing it up everywhere. Not only does this serve as a way of backing up the information so that it isn't lost, but the financial department doesn't need to go searching for files because it'll be on their computer and they can't change it once it is in there.

You Can Backup Blocks Or Blockchains Entirety

As already stated before, you can have different segments of information. You can have blockchains that are contained within blocks, which means you can make an entire database from just blockchain technology, get all of the security you would have from a blockchain, and have an ecosystem built around this.

No De-Platforming

What is De-Platforming?

De-platforming is the act of taking someone's platform away. As of writing this book, Patreon is in trouble with a YouTuber known as Sargon because they evicted him from their platform for off-platform behavior. Currently, people are leaving the website in droves and a few of the top earners are talking about creating their own service, but one thing has come up in all of them: cryptocurrency. Cryptocurrency removes the barrier of entry for many websites that want to exchange money. For instance, Patreon must work with PayPal in order to process transactions, PayPal has to go through Mastercard or Visa, then this goes through the ACH, and the goes back down the tree to finally get to the person that needs the money. That's about 4 gateways with 3 companies that could turn it down. With the blockchain and cryptocurrency, it's from the consumer to the provider. There is no middleman with cryptocurrency, which allows these companies to operate without needing approval from other competing companies.

Blockchain Cannot Be Blocked Directly

The best part about the entire process is that even if a company was told no by another company, they could still find another way to use the blockchain even without cryptocurrency. Cryptocurrency has no borders, which means that if the company can't get approval through PayPal then it can go through some other country's payment processor that's friendly that will then funnel money through the ACH. This effectively destroys any politically motivated company from denying a user money.

Blockchain Has No Borders

Cryptocurrency really has no borders, which means that blockchain has no borders. Imagine a country that was trying to get money for a revolution. Well, if the people had their money in paper form this could be confiscated and lost when an oppressive military invaded. Cryptocurrency is on the internet, which means they could easily save it to some online system far away from it being taken. Essentially, oppressive governments could never de-fund revolutionaries because that country would have to shut down the internet to do so and that can be detrimental to a country's economy.

For example, the economy of Egypt has been significantly impacted by a devaluation of their currency, among other factors ever since there have been significant restrictions on their use of the internet. Sure, there are other factors involved in the Egyptian economy, but the internet restriction is a contributor.

LIMITATIONS OF THE BLOCKCHAIN

Public Acceptance

People Generally Don't Understand Technology

Perhaps the most frustrating thing about everything is that for this to be useful it has to convince the public. For the majority of history, things are usually built with a use. Oftentimes, that use has to be plastered in front of the user's face several times before they understand the importance of it in their life. That doesn't mean that users are stupid, it just means that people, in general, have a very hard time changing their habits for the needs of the market as the market changes its habits for the needs of the customer.

This means that even though a technology is fantastic and has many applications, it does mean that they are also going to look at the technology like it's got a moral attitude. If trustworthy brands demean the value or associate the use of technology with criminal elements, they are more likely not to use it. Essentially, even though that tool is very useful, if a social association can be made that attaches that technology to something bad, then people are very mistrusting of the technology. You could explain it all day long, tell them about how fantastic it is, but until somebody they like endorses it you have a very small chance of getting them to go on board with it.

Campaigns from Competitors

There's a lot of money to be made by preventing blockchain from being implemented in the market. Remember that the blockchain does away with the middleman and there are entire companies dedicated to being a middleman. These middlemen have created campaigns to make a social association of a negative nature with blockchain to make sure that it doesn't take over the market.

For instance, the wealthiest middlemen are dealerships between the factory and the consumer. If blockchain technology is implemented with selling cars, dealerships will have a huge problem on their hands when consumers can bypass their monopoly-like laws to purchase brand new cars.

Most of what prevents a person from buying a brand-new car online is the fact that it is difficult to get it shipped to your house, it requires a lot of verification, and then it requires a lot of background fees. These companies make money from selling the car at a higher price than what the factory sells to them for and the interest rate on the monthly payments of the average car owner. They often hide in false promises such as if your car breaks down, they'll fix it only for the customer to find out later that they'll fix it if it broke down in a certain way. It's not necessarily a false promise, but it does come across as a false promise because that was not what was told to them but that was what was on paper. People often pay attention to what is sold to them via the voice rather than what's on the paper. To some people, it honestly feels like legal papers are made long and boring, so people sign on them without reading the fine print. That's just a small detail in the grand pattern of and all of these companies will generally get away with making tons of money without the consumer knowing until after they've had a horrible experience. This leaves only the customers who don't really need those extra benefits to promote the company so that more poor individuals have bad experiences.

These people don't like the fact that you can have a solid verification pattern with the blockchain. They need to verify your driver's license, your signature needs to be verified, they need to run a background check on your credit score which requires further identification, and by the end of it they have so much identification they may know more about you than many police officers or even the guy who stole your credit card sometime. All of this can be done online and over the blockchain.

If the government implements a lookup system for driver's license and incorporates some sort of login feature to prevent users outside of the network that are not trusted by the government to get in, any major seller like Amazon or Walmart could take your license number and run it against that database to verify your identity before having a customer support agent come online to record you as you sign a piece of paper saying you bought a car, which is then stored in that same blockchain that they did thousands of other customers along with the contract so that it'll never be lost. All of the information that the sales associate might need could be accessed via a blockchain, requiring no more than digital access. This is a very difficult case to fight for the existence of dealerships beyond being able to look in the car and feel the experience in the car. However, this is also defeated because now you can experience what it's like in a car by putting on a VR headset and sitting in a real-sized version of that car so that you can see what the car is like.

Enormous middlemen brands have begun to notice this and are campaigning to make blockchain look like it's the primary tool for criminals in an attempt to get the technology banned. It doesn't matter if the technology would make people's lives easier, more secure, and overall provide a better experience, it just matters that these companies continue making money without having to make any major changes. Companies do this all the time, with Apple practically being a spokesman about this with constant issues like suing products coming from China simply because they had an Apple logo on it, because it was a reused Apple part, trying to pass it off as fraud.

Cryptocurrency Bane

The sad thing is they don't need to do much work to get this point across. Cryptocurrency had a very large campaign against it by companies that support Fiat money. They would say things like it's criminal money or it's the money used on the dark web, which leads people to believe that it's a bad thing because they are bad people using it. To the average person who has an IQ more than their teenage kid, this is utter nonsense.

However, whether or not it is nonsense, a great majority of people believed it and that is the primary crux of the problem. A lot of people believe that cryptocurrency is a bad thing for a variety of problems. It's associated with criminals, it has an unpredictable stock market, and many other reasons caused people to veer away from cryptocurrency. The reason why this is the crux of the problem is because when people hear blockchain came from cryptocurrency, all those previous associations are now attached to the blockchain. This is a huge limitation for the technology and it works to the benefits of every company that would have automatically been affected by blockchain technology.

No Mainstream No Acceptance

All of this underpins the bigger problem and that is that it there is no mainstream support; companies will not support it. New companies and middle-sized companies are willing to endorse new technologies that look good on the company and they are often the great innovators that decide the next decade. Old and bigger companies want to downplay the technology as long as they can so that they can either keep their profits, switch over to the new technology while they can, or squash out the entire industry itself if they can't make that switch.

It's a repetitive pattern as all new companies either have to comply with what's currently being done or they have to fight the bigger companies, and this requires public approval. If the public does not support them, they will not win the fight and that means if blockchain is not supported by the mainstream public then blockchain will not be implemented in all the areas we know it can be because companies with mainstream public approval will be able to effectively fight it back.

Government Acceptance

Governments Are Slow

When it comes to practically anything, the government is slower than the slowest snail on the planet. Getting things done through the government takes years and sometimes even decades depending on the situation. Very rarely does a government conduct something that takes no less than six months because governments tend to spend their time arguing over the final details and ensuring that there isn't a vagueness to the law. This is highly beneficial because that means that laws can be challenged on specifics and then people from the public can challenge those laws if the specifics do not meet that government's own rules; a contradictory of terms.

The problem with which I'm pointing out here is the number of laws concerning blockchain because a great example is vaping from

111

2009. The American FCC and other regulatory bodies regrettably classified vaping or, rather, the products associated with vaping as tobacco related products. In a tobacco product such as a cigarette, one needs a way of lighting a fire and then the consumer will breathe in the smoke of the substance. In vaping, the coil that's wrapped around the cotton boils the electronic fluid otherwise known as e-liquid so that a vapor is produced that contains those chemicals. In the definition of science, the only two things that these two different categories of products have is that they are delivery systems and they deliver nicotine. In health, practice, and nearly everything else the two are completely different. Yet it took the government nearly a decade after the product hit the market to classify this substance and its delivery systems as tobacco-related, which many think is an incorrect classification. It took a decade to apply existing laws to a product. Imagine how long it would take for those various trust laws that are applicable to money and technology to be applied to cryptocurrency and the blockchain.

The Bane of Cryptocurrency on Blockchain

Those in the government are not exactly the brightest bulbs

when it comes to technology because it's not their job. Weather hasn't

been their job until the past two decades when it became extremely

relevant. In other words, most governmental leaders don't know about

technology because they really didn't grow up with it and it became a

tool for their professional life that didn't require them to know the

specifics. Professionals in the technology field handle those specifics

for them and this is the problem that we face with blockchain in the

governmental body.

Blockchain is confusing to entry-level programmers and yet

programmers would have been able to ask better questions than

Congress did of Mark Zuckerberg. So, to expect governmental bodies

do understand the concept is pushing it. Time after time after time, it's

been displayed that governmental entities that receive the limelight

often do not have the intellectual capacity for medium to advanced

technology. Hillary Clinton with her email server, the creation of a

cyber division department within the government after it was a threat

113

for three decades, and the multitude of other cyber security issues that have blasted news headings since the 1990s. People who have a political career, on the average, did not grow up with technology and tend to have very little experience with technology.

Difficult to Regulate

Not only that is but blockchain technology morphs every year. Bitcoin blockchain is different than Etherium blockchain and so on and so forth. How can you make a consistent set of federal laws that the blockchain and users of the blockchain can commit to if it changes every single time you have enough time to make a law about it? It is incredibly difficult to regulate the use of a blockchain and because blockchain updates as fast as a neurotic programmer can code a new application, it is nigh impossible to define the blockchain when the blockchain has variations.

The point of it being difficult to regulate is actually an internet-wide trend because many of the laws that are applicable to the internet in the country are not necessarily applicable to all countries. This is actually to the detriment of the user experience because what winds up happening is that companies, in an effort to easily conform to the law, use the most difficult to follow rules to set the guidelines on their platform. For instance, when the European Union came out with a new directive the giant websites of Google, Facebook, YouTube, Twitter and the like all updated their terms of service at the same to and it happened to be almost identical to that of the new directive. In other words, if you want to use YouTube you almost have to follow the exact same rules as those in Europe. International law has now superseded sovereign law via the Internet because it's easier for companies to conform to that.

Difficult to Monitor

The last part is the concept of being able to monitor the activity to ensure laws are being followed. Several times we have seen the government try to overstep its bounds and tell companies to lower their encryption standards because the government can't break it. What do you think is going to happen with blockchain technology?

The purpose of the government is to have control over its citizens for the most part. So when it comes to things like police officers and following the law, the government likes to claim that it needs an eye on everything to make sure that everything is being followed to the letter. Even in a country like America where it used to be the distance between homes that insured privacy, encryption ensures privacy online yet the government previously found it easier to have things like cities so that both houses and businesses could be located in the same spot just as it is easier to have encryption that isn't really difficult to break. There really is no excuse for the government asking for a way to decrypt something when that ability in it of itself defeats the purpose of encrypting. For example, if revolutionaries in the past that overthrew oppressive governments had those governments listen in on every conversation, those governments would not have been overthrown. In other words, encryption is another form of protecting the individual from the government and the government doesn't like that. So what's to say that the government, when it makes laws regulating the blockchain, won't try to build in a backdoor like they did with laws concerning technology products in workstations, they've been trying to do with smartphone companies, and consistently try with internet service providers?

Financial Institution Acceptance

Cryptocurrency Has Proven to Be Unstable

Once again, we have to tie this back to cryptocurrency because cryptocurrency and the blockchain have not been separated into their own entities in the eyes of the public. Just as I had mentioned before that negative perception of cryptocurrency bleeds into the perception of the blockchain, so too does the perception of cryptocurrency be unstable. Cryptocurrency is notorious for both jumping up in value and drastically decreasing in value for seemingly no reason at all. In most market trends, you can predict when a company might get a lot of money and might lose a lot of money, but the existence of the Dogecoin is proof enough that something that no one thought would have value has value in the cryptocurrency market.

Knowing about how unstable cryptocurrency has been, it is difficult to get someone to understand that while cryptocurrency uses the blockchain, cryptocurrency is not the blockchain. The technology industry has a huge problem with technophobia by people in power. People who have been in power for more than 50 years, whether it is commercial or governmental, very rarely understand how technology works and usually mistrust technology. It is so common in society that it has actually become a stereotype of anyone over a certain age. Yet, those people tend to be the true leaders of very important industries.

It Takes IT to Explain it

To make it even worse is that an IT professional usually has to explain what the differences are. This may not seem like a problem to IT professionals until you realize that the vast majority of businesses underestimate the importance of the IT position. There are countless examples of businesses hiring a freelance developer to build their website so that it looks and functions the way that they want it to. They then do not keep that freelancer on for maintaining and updating that software. This problem is getting better, but it is still bad. Most companies do not have a maintenance team, most of the companies that do have a maintenance team consider their maintenance team to be the IT support that a company like Squarespace or HostGator provides. The problem with a service like Squarespace is that even though they can provide security, they can also, potentially, make you more vulnerable because if they get hacked you get hacked. The only difference in that situation is that if they get hacked, every company associated with them also gets hacked, leading to tons of websites getting hacked all at once and the incentive to do so is much higher. It is a huge security flaw that most businesses that are hiring in the commercial food chain realize and is the reason why they tend to not use them. There are other reasons, but that is a linchpin reason.

Companies are hiring freelancers to create their own form of cryptocurrency because they know how much money can be made from it. When it takes an IT professional to explain it you have to consider the ignorance of the average consumer that's going to use it. Not everyone uses SolidWorks or AutoCAD yet the two programs are quintessential in our functioning society. Yet many people have only ever heard of one of them and have only ever heard it in passing. These are software that build the buildings they live in and build the parts that are in practically all of their products, yet they are names that would be lost on the vast majority of them. The blockchain is a very similar type of technology with the ability to replace most of how everything functions in society yet if you ever bring up the blockchain to anyone that was an average consumer and not in financial, marketing, business management, or a programmer they would understand you better if you talked about Bitcoin.

It Takes Cooperation

Perhaps the worst part about this is that you have to cooperate on multiple fronts for this technology to even have a purpose. For instance, in the car dealership example you have to have the car manufacturer to agree to use your system, you have to have the local governments agree to your system, you have to have the credit union agree to your system, you have to have your system inspected to ensure compliance with the existing laws, and you have to have a buyer willing to purchase from that ecosystem at the bare minimum. There's so much that you have to have cooperating with you that if any one of those fail it is almost unviable to actually implement a business based off of it.

Not only this but you also have to have a system that people can understand because if you leave it to a programmer to name things then only the programmer and the people who talk to the programmer would understand the purpose of those names. Therefore, you have to have a content designer and sales marketer that are also able to understand how the blockchain works in your ecosystem just to make the website understandable and functional. It is an incredibly enormous task to take on but that doesn't mean it's not worth doing it because the first person that does take on this issue and succeeds will find themselves as one of the top in their industry.

It Takes Mainstream

Last but not least is the news cycle. The news cycle is a bought Enterprise and I mean to say that those who own these news companies are often people in positions who own your competitors. What you will find is that if you try to go up against them, they will use everything in their power to give you as much bad PR as possible and trying to block every financial path that you have.

A good example of this is a company that was a startup known as Subscribe Star. Subscribe Star is a competitor of Patreon.

Patreon made an ideologically political move in many people's opinions against the Republican side in America and so some quickly looked to Subscribe Star as an alternative. Also, as soon as Subscribe Star got going, PayPal decided to quit its involvement with the company; almost as if there was some sort of communication between PayPal and Patreon. Therefore, the company had customers but have no way to receive the money essentially killing them as a company. As of writing this book the situation is still being handled and we will see what will come of this, but it serves as an example of what happens when these competitors try to target you.

Breaking the Mechanism

Users Are Still Lazy

The primary problem with securing information online is that users are incredibly lazy to a degree that would amaze most people. You see, user input, as much as it's needed in order to actually be the product, creates an encryption problem magnitude higher than most people understand. Most people understand that when you use a password several times, it's very easy for a person to figure out what your password likely is. It's the reason why there's an online list of the most commonly used passwords because, again, people are incredibly lazy. What happens is that if you know that a user goes to this website and then goes to another website but uses the same password or has a high likelihood of using the same password for both of them, you can actually figure out what the password is based off of which letters are different from each other. No matter how you encrypt something, if the password is the same you can create a mathematical differentiation between the two and effectively break both encryptions by having the same password in different encryption methods.

123

A huge problem with the entire blockchain being encrypted is that someone else can figure out how it's encrypted if you don't handle it correctly. You can figure out how it's encrypted in very much the same way that I just described to you because if a user's name is the same as the previous users name and the users name before that, what happens is that a whole bunch of users names will pile up that are the same and if a person has access to that they can then run it against names with the same amount of letters. The name was a central source of why the encryption was broken. Using the same encryption pattern will create an encryption that is identical in every single situation and then the person can reverse-engineer how you got to that point of encryption. It takes a significant amount of time to do this, but it's not anywhere near the level of Brute Force breaking an encryption should take.

Using the blockchain because it's an encryption method is an experimental technology because unless you are able to cordon off blockchains then the entire blockchain is open. When the entire blockchain is open you then risk the problem of someone getting access and then being able to figure it out based off of these factors.

Essentially getting access to the usernames and passwords or perhaps

the real identities of these people very quickly. Therefore, sensitive

information can be leaked online almost as easily as someone making a

backdoor into a database. The primary difference here is that unlike

making a back door into a database, blockchain allows a user to create

modular parts that can use different encryption patterns based on the

module that it's in. What this does is it blurs the encryption method and

makes it so that it is significantly more difficult to break the encryption.

So, to give you an example, let's take those two names again and say

that they are the same name but with different encryption methods.

Unless you know specifically that those are two of the same names, the

only way that you can figure out that they are the same names is the

number of unchanging letters and the commonality of letters. The

commonality of letters refers to the frequency in which we use the

letters in our alphabet. I think the most commonly used letter is an e and

that is because it is very common in everyday words but vowels, in

general, are the most commonly used letters in the English alphabet.

Knowing this, you can figure out which ones are vowels if there are enough letters in a name. There are ways around it but by using two different encryption methods, a direct comparison cannot be made and so the reverse engineering process would require brute-forcing both encryption methods rather than finding a mathematical differentiation between the two.

Encryption is a Delay Tactic

Having said that, a lot of people have this misconception that encryption is a permanent guard against people who want to get at sensitive information. These usually involve people who are outside of the tech industry and don't really think about how information is secured on a daily basis. In other words, the vast majority of society doesn't actually understand how information is regularly secured on different platforms.

Those that are in the tech industry understand that encryption is really a delay tactic and we are getting better at increasing the amount of delay that there is. For instance, the first most common form of encryption that we know of is actually known as rot13 and this is because Julius Caesar used it whenever he would send out messages that needed to be encrypted. Once you understood how this encryption method worked it would be really quick to figure out what the contents of a message was but until then no one had used encryption and so no one could figure out what messages meant.

Nowadays, the same thing can be done with current encryption methods and the only difference is in the amount of time it takes to do just that. Encryption is a method of hiding information by combining different elements together. Once you know what those elements are, it's a matter of running through the different combinations to figure out the exact combination that you used to encrypt all your stuff. Therefore, when it comes to encryption it's really just extending the amount of time that it takes a CPU to run through the combinations required to find the one combination that will be used to break your encryption pattern.

HOW TO OVERCOME THESE

Educating the Public

Don't Primarily Focus on Adults

When it comes to educating the public a lot of people like to say that we need more young adults to learn this material so that it's quickly applicable. The problem is that a little bit too much is focused on teaching adults because adults are not generally going to experience the blockchain boom.

To understand this, you have to look at the smartphone because smartphones are really a relatively new concept. Starting in the year 2001 with Japan being the front-runner for them and we began to see them at around 2006 in the U.S. It took nearly a decade for everyone to really have a smartphone because what happens is that expensive technology is adopted by those who can afford it and then the popularity causes companies to create cheaper forms of it. This means that the blockchain, which is still a rather obscure technology, is still in the stages of the cell phone era.

Cell phones have been around for far longer than smartphones and it was because it didn't require much for cell phones to be created. It doesn't require much for a cryptocurrency and blockchain to be created. However, it did require a lot of expensive upfront cost for you to justify the need for a cell phone and as we progressed to the smartphone, we began to see cell phones at reasonable prices for the first few years before smartphones really hit the market. Once smartphones hit the market, cell phones were almost immediately made obsolete as a result of this.

Cryptocurrency started in the early 2010s with its invention going back much further, which represents a similar trend line in terms of creation. The concept and the first creation of cryptocurrencies was about two decades before we really saw something as big as Bitcoin. It was an academic idea for the most part, but once Bitcoin hit the market it began to accrue a lot of popularity once it had value and people knew it was easy to obtain. Now that Bitcoin has had a time to have its boom, what we are seeing now is that Bitcoin is slowly coming back down to its normal stabilized level. This is known as a crash for people because they didn't see it coming nor were they able to prepare for it. Blockchain technology is a specific component of cryptocurrency just as cell phones are a specific component of smartphone technology. It has taken a number of years to go from the blockchain as we knew it with Bitcoin to the Smart Contracts that we know with Etherium. Within about a decade we will see blockchain technology being used within companies and being almost as pervasive as smartphones have become now, but professional adults that could use this right now won't feel the effect until about a decade from now. This means that teaching young adults about this really teaches the 30-40-year olds how to get along with blockchain world.

Put It In Teen Products

To really have a decent effect, you need to affect the teen market. Cell phones did not expand as much as they did because of adults because adults tended to use cell phones as a utility and adults still tend to use smartphones as utilities. The ones that made it fashionable to have a new smartphone every year were the teens that grew up getting smartphones handed down to them from adults. After all, you don't exactly just want to throw away a $300 piece of hardware. Your teenager might get some use out of it so why not hand it down? Essentially, smartphones began to explode very quickly because the teenage population got to have their hands on them at an early age and then began to expect them as they became teenagers.

To have people understand what blockchain can do for you is a requirement of making the blockchain something that teens can use. Now, the average person will not understand what that means but considering the vast majority of encryption did messages are utilized by the teenage age group and young adults, you can begin to understand how to implement it with teenagers.

The reason why teenagers are so important is because teenagers are incredibly social. At that point they have a mixture of trying to get with their friends but also wanting to be able to afford their own items.

Essentially, they are their own advertisement at that point in time and they are able to maintain a level of income that can usually be spent on expensive products. Cryptocurrency was a very popular tagline in YouTube videos a few short years ago because there was a lot of interest in generating money with cryptocurrency, not with adults but with teenagers and young adults. This is because teenagers and young adults had money to spend, to waste, which meant that a lot of investment went in to cryptocurrency with these teenagers and young adults. This was a form of making teenagers open to the idea of cryptocurrency and now we have an entire generation that has seen the benefit of cryptocurrency and the potential problems with cryptocurrency.

The reason why this is important is because teenagers will be the ones that fix the problems of the past so any problems that teenagers experience with cryptocurrency now, teenagers will be able to fix when they enter the job market. Introducing the blockchain to teenagers introduces them to the benefits and the problems of blockchain technology, which represents an opportunity to implement blockchain into an expected form of life. By doing this, blockchain can very quickly obtain popularity and products that utilize blockchain will be popular amongst teenagers. By advertising and educating teenagers, companies will be forced into implementing blockchain technology as a way to compete with other companies that are utilizing the teenage fascination with blockchain technology. This has actually been seen in marketing advertisements that use the word gamer.

They use the word gamer because for some reason the marketers see a 20% increase when the word is used, regardless of whether that keyboard is the same as a regular keyboard. You can have a keyboard that is generic and then you could have a keyboard that's labeled gamer and the one that has the gamer label will do 20% better. This is because teenagers don't really think too hard about the specifics of a product, they think a lot about The Branding and what it means to have that product. Therefore, while someone might think that Logitech is the best keyboard on the planet because it's got a smart screen built into it, a Chinese manufacturer who comes out with an RGB keyboard that took maybe $10 to make can sell more because it's associated with the brand of gamers and being a gamer is something Logitech doesn't advertise. This makes it relatable to teenagers and with teenagers, the most crucial selling aspect is how it relates to the teenager's life. By teaching teenagers what blockchain technology is and how it can be used in their life, you effectively motivate the market to develop better more complicated forms of blockchain to increase the benefits that blockchain can provide.

Teach the Kids

To go even further than that you need to teach the kids because the kids will be the ones who become teenagers and see the problems that the teenagers cause. The best way to understand this is the gaming industry itself. If we were to rewind by about 21 years, we will be introduced to what most considered to be the best beginning to the gaming area that there was and that was the late 1990s. During the late 1990s, you had consoles that were coming out like the PS2 and the Xbox and games that had stayed with kids during that time until now. As time has progressed, those games have gotten more graphically and programmatically more complex and better in some cases. Storytelling has pretty much stayed the same and it's really just the graphical details that have changed along with how much you can interact with. Those systems inspired the kids who are making games now, games like Red Dead Redemption 2 and Spider-Man and those are some of the highest selling games of the year this book is written in. The problem is that the AAA industry has a really bad reputation at the moment because somewhere along the way, smartphones were invented and free games had microtransactions in them to make profit off of free games. If you think about how microtransactions are the bane of current video game technology in terms of making money, you can actually think microtransactions are really good because they tend to make a lot of money.

The problem with that way of thinking is that you sacrifice the enjoyment of video games with every microtransaction you shove into your game. These kids who are playing games as adults experienced a time where there were no microtransactions. They make games for the story and the enjoyment of video games, which means the Indie Market that was small many years ago has now exploded with video game makers who grew up during that time.

Along the way, video games became a form of making money rather than an art form. Video game companies that were making the biggest games playable, the ones developed on the PS2, stayed around and began incorporating people who grew up with microtransactions inside of free games. These same people have company leaders who try to exploit every single way of making money possible yet now we are seeing trends in video games in the AAA gaming sometimes doing worse than Indie Games. A great example of this is Five Nights at Freddy's, which made some of the highest game sales of all time with Indie Games and competed with a lot of AAA industry games. So you have a cross between those that grew up poor wanting to make the most money and those that grew up with the vision of beautiful and impactful video games crossing paths within the same industry.

Teenagers will use blockchain technology in order to do certain things that they're probably not supposed to do and make transactions with people in other countries as we come online more often. Kids will look at how teenagers are making use of the blockchain technology and they will find something wrong with that use, which further opens up the possibilities of what blockchain can do. Once kids and teenagers understand what blockchain technology is and purchase more products with it, you will see companies quickly conform to using blockchain in every aspect of their company that they can benefit for themselves but they will also realize the marketing benefits that come with saying that their technology is what the teenagers and kids want.

Working within The Loopholes

Open Companies in Digitally Unregulated Areas

Facebook and YouTube are fantastic examples of companies opening businesses in areas that are not normally heavily regulated. Facebook was a social interaction platform that allowed people to connect to each other long before it became the tangled web that it is now. YouTube used to be a very small video website that had incredibly small videos on it with a small percentage of society even knowing it existed. That was almost a decade ago and now they are among the biggest companies in the world while just now facing the curtails of regulation in the works.

You see, most communication when it came to forums and instant messengers went unregulated because it was actually pretty small and fell under the guise of free speech. For instance, let's say that you wanted to start a forum for everyone who really liked to build printed circuit boards. The only way that someone could be allowed into the group is if you invited them into the group and then, as the Forum owner, you could kick people out you didn't want in there and they couldn't do anything against you. Now, a lot of people don't realize that this is essentially the concept of Facebook and Twitter. Facebook and Twitter are two online forums that are extremely convenient and so a lot of people use them. Twitter is an open forum for the most part and recently started adding the ability to privatize your messages so that your personalized forum could only be seen by people who you approved to follow you. Facebook has been a closed forum for a very long time with public posting, which meant you could have private messages while also being able to post to the public.

Apply Blockchain in Less Known Industries

The Raspberry Pi is an excellent invention of ingenuity and planning as it serves as a device for various purposes. It was the original single board computer that provided a lot of uses and gained a lot of popularity. The mainstream public didn't know about the Raspberry Pi for a very long time and the first way that it was actually handed out was when you bought a magazine. Over time, it evolved into a usable single-board computer for everyday tasks except for gaming and hardware intensive applications like Adobe Premiere Pro. You could use it as a document editor, programming machine, or anything that just required low-level computing power.

The reason why I bring up the Raspberry Pi is because it's a lot like the blockchain. The blockchain started out as a very simple idea and has had its evolutions over the past few years. The Raspberry Pi is practically known to most parents that are not minimum wage because

139

it's a fantastic gift and project depending on how you want to handle it and it doesn't require a lot of experience. The blockchain, on the other hand, is still rather unknown to people and is not exactly user-friendly when it comes to explaining it. The Raspberry Pi represents a very lesser-known industry because the Raspberry Pi is not the only single board computer. Sure, it might have been the first, but it definitely isn't the only one that there is. In fact, there are a number of single board computers that are as powerful if not more powerful than the current release of Raspberry Pi. The only difference is that the Raspberry Pi had released in a lesser-known industry at the time and paved the way for the rest of these models. The blockchain can do the very same thing if it's given the opportunity.

For instance, why not develop a library system that bases itself off of the blockchain? Essentially, you just put an RFID chip inside of each book and it checks books in and out based on what's on the RFID chip and in the blockchain. Everyone knows what a library is but not many people actually know how the systems in the library function which means that they could be a useful way of expanding the control for blockchain. It would also give them a much better PR personality versus the criminal and unstable vision that cryptocurrency gives it.

Blockchain Implementation Via Creeping

That's the problem with today's generation, they expect change to happen overnight because they've seen it before. They've seen Lindsey Stirling up on the stage singing her heart out only to fail within a few months on the show she was singing for, yet she becomes an international star during the same time span. Justin Bieber was a similar story and this trend happens more often now than it ever did because once something is on the internet, it can spread like wildfire.

The problem is that this is not how new technology should be introduced. Most of everyone, as of writing this book, thinks that the world of VR is currently dead but it's not and it's actually expanding, it's just expanding at a very slow rate. Blockchain should be a technology that expands slowly because the slower something moves; the less people notice it moving at all. This means that eyes will not be placed on the blockchain until the blockchain has a secure foothold in society.

Believe it or not, this is how coding libraries work. A few years ago, no one knew what bootstrap was, a few years ago no one knew what react.js was, but they slowly made their way into the eyes of programmers and it became an adopted norm. Frameworks and Technology that's not seen as a good change by those competing with it should move at a very slow pace because if it moves fast then it won't be able to handle the challenges.

This means that the best way to really spread blockchain is to find some mundane use that it can have inside of your business. Perhaps you might want to create an instant messaging app that everyone at the business can use to communicate with each other and you just so happened to build it on the blockchain. Perhaps you want to clock the break times that people have and you build that on blockchain. Building small things out of blockchains will cause a very slow overtake of the current system that's in place. As it is said, a crab that is slowly brought to boil will not know that it is dying.

Setting Up the Finance Details and Security

A lot of the software that the finance industry uses is pretty much capitalized on because finance doesn't really change that much. I mean, a mortgage is still a mortgage, a loan is still a loan, buy and sell options are still buy and sell options, and the problem is that it's so slow in updating as an industry as a whole.

That isn't to say that Finance isn't a workable field and that isn't to say that there aren't updates made to the field, but the software around what a finance person does is pretty standard and doesn't really expand a whole lot because while there's an almost limitless product line money is still money.

Having said that, Finance deals in a lot of information that's sensitive. A company checking account number as well as the password to get in said checking account is not really something a company wants to share with other people. When someone goes about making changes to company accounts, this is yet another form of finance. A huge problem in company finance is determining how much money has been

143

spent and the blockchain technology can actually help mitigate

situations in which employees spend money on the company's behalf

without the company's permission. You see, the way the situation

normally goes is that an employee gets a card to spend it on certain

items like gas but then they will accompany those items with food or

drink at gas stations or even have a payout at the gas station. The way

they usually get caught is at the end of the year when they're required to

put in their receipt or at the end of the week, it's kind of obvious that

one of the receipts is not going to be like the others.

The problem is that this could actually be stopped before it

happens with an authorization card. An authorization card is a

middleman of sorts but digitally and this refers to a card that you swipe

at a credit card reader, but before the transaction goes through it is

actually sent to a separate station for approval before the transaction is

allowed. What occurs is that the authorization card requests the receipt

to be transmitted digitally and then the person on the other end can

approve or deny a transaction based upon what they read in the receipt.

In other words, it would stop employees from stealing from the company on the spot. The employee would then be responsible for paying for the items that they tried to use the company money on.

How does this involve the blockchain though? Well, the same authorization card can be used to automatically collect the receipts of employees that you can trust (or your own transactions). The time, the place, and similar things can be stored in an authorization request and you would want to keep this information and easily something that you want to have an easy look up for. It is very difficult to navigate a database if there's no way to make sure that it's segregated so you could separate each transaction by company, which would effectively ensure that known restaurants or manufacturers could proceed with the transaction without having to wait for an approval, while gas cards could be cordoned off into their own section. This would keep a better record of all transactions instead of receipts, prevent company theft/embezzlement, and help to ensure the accuracy and speed of tax specialists.

CONCLUSION

Blockchain Is A Powerful Technology

Blockchain is a really powerful technology and can be used for quite a lot, but the problem isn't that it's a powerful technology but a difficult to understand technology. Oftentimes, the blockchain itself needs a very lengthy article or book in order to describe its power and its uses. However, powerful technology is still powerful technology, by explaining it we only increase the amount of access people have to the power of this technology. It is very important to understand that with powerful technology does come a greater amount of responsibility for ensuring that everyone knows the truth about it because what happens is that people fearmonger very easily.

Fear-mongering has been a part of human Society for as long as recorded history, from the Kraken to the Devilry in Books. This has never ended, and it happens with everything that's new. Everything that's new is called a detriment to society until everyone has it and then everyone thinks it's weird that it was called a detriment to society.

Books were exclaimed to be the worst thing one could do to oneself and

now the biggest Business Leaders in the world are exclaiming that they

read at least one book a day. Right now, the digital age is upon us and

the time in which we figure out what we're going to do with the internet

now that it is a global society is considered to be the current detriment

to society. People will get along more if they would just get off the

internet except that the internet is no different than talking to a random

stranger. People will get along more if video games stop being so

violent; except that terrorism has always existed and that it hasn't really

increased or decreased in the wake of video games. There's always

science and logic to beat these down but fear-mongering always exists

and so it is the responsibility of those that love this technology, this new

invention to spread that explanation across the world so that we as a

society can improve.

A World Devoid of Middlemen

This isn't about the blockchain, I mean it really is about the blockchain, but it isn't that the blockchain will solve all the problems it will just solve the middleman problem. With a blockchain you no longer need a guy at a dealership to sell you a car, you no longer need a cashier at the register to check to see if you purchased that item in your hands, you no longer need someone to check identification at the bar, and you no longer need to worry about whether your shipment arrived or not. The middleman is a specialized industry that simply exists as a means of making sure that we trust one another and considering that the internet is a global marketplace, trust should be as digital as the internet itself. We should not have to rely on another person to decide we trust information but rather the mathematical proofs that have always served science well.

Printed in July 2019
by Rotomail Italia S.p.A., Vignate (MI) - Italy